The Granny Nanny

The Granny Nanny

✦

Conscious Grandmothering or What Every Grandmother Should Know About Babysitting

Lois Young-Tulin

iUniverse, Inc.

New York Lincoln Shanghai

The Granny Nanny
Conscious Grandmothering or What Every Grandmother Should Know About Babysitting

Copyright © 2005 by Lois Young-Tulin

iUniverse books may be ordered through booksellers or by contacting:

iUniverse
2021 Pine Lake Road, Suite 100
Lincoln, NE 68512
www.iuniverse.com
1-800-Authors (1-800-288-4677)

ISBN-13: 978-0-595-35188-6 (pbk)
ISBN-13: 978-0-595-67211-0 (cloth)
ISBN-13: 978-0-595-79884-1 (ebk)
ISBN-10: 0-595-35188-3 (pbk)
ISBN-10: 0-595-67211-6 (cloth)
ISBN-10: 0-595-79884-5 (ebk)

Printed in the United States of America

Dedication

For my grandchildren—the personification of possibilities and hope—who help make my life fulfilling:

Dylan, Jasper, Felix and Rachael—and Barak and Terri's expected baby girl—and Nick and Bennett—and future grandchildren yet to come...

Thank you to the many women interviewed for this book, their openness, their love, their friendship and their Granny Nanny status.

The stories shared in this book are about real people and the actual things they said; however, names have been changed and care has been taken to protect the actual identities of the people who requested anonymity.

Contents

Introduction

When I learned that my older son and his wife were expecting a baby, I thought long and hard about the role that I wanted to play in my grandchild's life. I also examined my image of grandmother—a grey-haired senior citizen, knitting sweaters and going out to lunch. I never knew my paternal grandmother, but my maternal grandmother lived with us and baked wonderful pies. My own mother was special to my children. Her home always smelled delicious and was a welcoming haven for my children.

I suspected that I was to face a unique opportunity as a grandmother, an opportunity to pass on my attitudes and skills to a future generation. An opportunity to enrich my life as well as to impact the lives of my children and grandchildren. This, I suspected, was the beginning of a new period in my life, a time when my family would expand and new memories would be formed.

But, I wondered, was I up to the task? Did I want to play a key role in my grandchildren's lives? Would I be a willing baby sitter? Would I find a balance between meddling and being aloof?

All these thoughts led me to explore the experiences of other grandmothers and to envision the grandmother I strove to be. As I interviewed over forty women, I came up with the concept of the Granny Nanny—what to me was the ideal grandmother. Having successfully raised three children of my own, I assumed I had the skills to be an effective, baby-sitting grandma. Little did I know how much child rearing techniques had changed.

The Granny Nanny offers hints on grandmothering and skills grandmothers must master to best nurture and love their grandchildren. In addition, one interviewed grandmother led me to another as the grandmother network spread and grew, encompassing nearby and long distance grandmothers, divorced grandmothers, step grannies, gay grannies, chosen grandmas, and even live-in grandmothers.

The openness of the grandmothers with whom I spoke was both astonishing and invaluable. Even long distance grandmothers, with consciously planned regular visits, play an important role in their grandchildren's lives. Many of the women with whom I spoke offered helpful hints on how to enhance their grandmothering roles—hints that I am sure will help other grandmothers fulfill their roles.

Personally, I learned a great deal from these women. I try to incorporate their suggestions into my relationships with my grandchildren, children and in-laws. My hope is that readers of *The Granny Nanny* will find the information from baby proofing your house to the paternal versus the maternal grandmother helpful as they become Granny Nannies and make memories with their grandchildren.

1

I'm A Grandmother!
or
What Were We Thinking?

Think about it. In order to be grandmothers we once had to be mothers. After giving birth, we, as the mothers, were responsible for our baby's/child's well being. As grandmothers, on the other hand, we have choices. Our roles are open for interpretation and conscious choices. When I became a grandmother, and even when my daughters-in-law were pregnant, I made a conscious decision to be an involved grandmother, one of the caretakers or a Granny-Nanny.

I was sure that helping out and taking care of a baby would be easy like getting back on a bicycle after a twenty-year lapse. Oh, how wrong I was. There are new rules, new products, new findings and plenty of taboos. How did my three children ever survive their hazardous childhoods?

Let's begin with car rides. There was the old car bed to put my infants in when they were little or someone's lap, safely held in loving arms. No! I learned. Regulation car seats are not only required, but hospitals will not send babies home unless the transporting car has the proper car seat inside. Not only did my children forego seatbelts, they weren't even regulation equipment in the old trusty station wagon. I remember that as toddlers they would stand behind me as I drove, their heads not even reaching the roof of the car. How did they ever survive? And worst of all, I used to smoke...yes, in the car! Today I'd be arrested. But, of course, I long kicked that filthy habit.

I was lucky. They survived these treacherous rides and arrived home from various outings in time for their naps. Stomach down they slept like little angels. Stomach down is verboten! Babies must sleep on their backs. They even sell spe-

3

cial guards to prevent the babies from turning over voluntarily onto their stomachs from their backs. And the dreaded SIDS statistics have improved as a result of these back-sleepers. Of course, crawling is more difficult for these back loungers, and their arms do not always get the needed strength necessary for other creeping games. But they live! What was I thinking?

While my little angels slept, I was busy sterilizing bottles. "What's that?" my daughter-in-law asks. No more sterilizing. Babies need to build up resistance to germs, just clean out the bottles…actually, throw out the plastic liners that hold the formula, and rinse the nipples and caps and you're done. Time to get the cloth diapers ready for the diaperman's pick-up and delivery. Diaperman? What's that? Disposable diapers rule! How easy feeding and coming out the other end is today.

My babies lived most of their days in stretch suits with snappable bottoms. Today's babies are models…you heard me, designer models. Baby Gap, Tommy Hilfiger, outfits to die for. Most of these outfits, by the way, were gifts since parents more often than not register on-line for baby gifts. Before my grandson even saw the light of day he had all the equipment, clothes, toys and books his parents had registered for him. Now that I would have liked! I remember receiving some horrendous outfits that were unreturnable, or triples and doubles of other things, and who had the time to return items when you're busy sterilizing bottles and washing diapers?

Crying! I remember the pediatrician telling me that each baby has a fussy period and that parents have to let their babies cry. Good exercise, they counseled. Untrue! Babies cry for a reason, I now learn. Try checking diapers, sleep patterns, hunger, anything because the baby knows best. Demand feeding has replaced scheduled feeding.

Water was introduced gently to baby. The bath! Any other water like a pool should be avoided. No longer. Mommies are taking their babies for swimming lessons as early as six months old.

Remember the word "no"? Forget it! No is too negative. Parents today distract. The key is DISTRACTION, rather than negative warnings. Okay, except if it's a dangerous situation, I'm sure I will lose it and yell, "No!" God help me.

A baby slept through the night once solid food was introduced. Hold it! Don't go so fast! Babies don't get solid food until at least the five-month mark. So what if you are a zombie from those middle-of-the-night feedings, ALLERGIES must be caught. Food is introduced slowly, food by food, taste by taste, slowly. And don't be sharing your table food so fast.

In the beginning, our pediatrician made house calls until the baby was strong enough to come out to the office and sit in the waiting room with other children, some sick and catchy. No more! House calls, what are they? Right away pack up the baby, put him or her into that complicated car seat that you need a doctorate to figure out, and rain or snow, like a mail carrier, carry your baby to the doctor.

Pacifiers are more acceptable, but only dental-correct pacifiers, specially shaped to prevent the teeth from growing in wrong. Maybe that's why all three of my children had to endure braces. What did I know?

Remember the term babysitter? Well, don't call one so fast, they can be child beaters, monsters, strangers. Take those babies with you to weddings, movies, any place rather than trust a non-family member to watch your baby, unless it's a bonded day care center. That's another story and costs almost as much as a state college's tuition.

I know that, as my grandsons grow, so will the new rules meet me square in the face. No more sending your toddlers out to play…dangerous! Children playing outside with friends can get kidnapped. Forget it! And strangers are to be avoided, watched, warned against. Be thankful today if your child is unfriendly, one never knows what lurks in the shadows of a shopping mall.

And what's with all this asthma? Look in the coatroom of any pre-school and you'll see inhalators lined up in the cubbies. Incidences of asthma are up…way up! Don't trust a kid who doesn't have a touch of asthma.

Now…summer comes, and your little swimmer is kicking up a storm but beware of that sun! The sun is our enemy; the ozone layer (whatever that is) has been destroyed. Make sure your child is well covered, hat, shirt, sunscreen above 115, sunglasses. Don't be so quick with those pails and shovels on the beach, the sun will bake their little bodies.

It's a brand new playing field for tomorrow's leaders. And we can watch their progress instantly…with those special cameras hooked up to our computers; my son e-mails to me daily photographs of baby Dylan. I love it! No waiting for film to be developed or envelopes to be mailed with treasured photos inside.

Speaking of my son, and all of our sons! Aren't they unbelievable? Daddies are as involved as mommies these days and I love it. I remember my husband yelling for me when confronted with a full diaper. I remember how only my ears heard a child wake up in the middle of the night. Today it's an even playing field. Mommies and Daddies work, they change diapers, they do everything for the baby…equally. It's about time!

As my grandsons grow I expect to be learning a lot more about the new parenting. Time out…I've heard of it, I've even watched my neighbor enforce

Time-Out! I'm sure I'll be instructed on that as the proper road to discipline. But if I were one of these toddlers being given Time-Out, I'd love it. Just look into one of those children's rooms…electronic toys, full libraries, toys for the dolls, busy boxes, creative activities. Time out to view all those wonderful videos for kids. Time-Out doesn't seem like jail to me.

Let's talk about helmets. Scooters, tricycles, bicycles…no more skinned knees. Today's kids don helmets and body pads before mounting their scooters or cycles. We were dumb parents in the old days. I have added to my prayers a special thanks to the gods for sparing my kids as they blithely wore shorts, their hair blowing in the breeze and their skin turning bronze as they pedaled around the neighborhood. What were we thinking?

I have a lot to learn from my parent/children. They know what they are doing. Dr. Spock used to tell mothers like me to follow our instincts, be natural. What did he know? I'm only grateful that my children survived the stupid way I raised them, hit and miss, lots of love, and after a good supper the prize maraschino cherry from the top of the cake. Only kidding! Back then we already knew about that deadly red dye, and those delicious unnatural red cherries were banned from our diets. After all I wasn't completely stupid, but actually an avid environmentalist, which, by the way, might have been why disposable diapers weren't very popular…think of the pollution and waste of natural resources. We recycled our cloth diapers.

I was also against war, and my children's toys were peaceful, no guns or GI Joes for my sons; as well as a women's libber…dolls for the boys, and my daughter played with trucks. Our house rang with the sounds of the songs from the album "Free To Be You and Me" and a well-worn recording of the song "I Am Woman."

Come to think of it, maybe that's one of the reasons why my sons are such involved Daddies and my daughter has such a successful professional life. Once they got over the hump of physical danger, they forged ahead to become the super parents that they are today. And I smile to myself every time I turn on the television and see that Mr. Rogers and Sesame Street are still the rage. Now there are two old pals that have survived the generations. Maybe we did something right that hasn't been thrown out with the bath water.

Now, lo and behold! Son #2 and his wife, both working parents, gave birth to a boy, and 15 months later to another boy. They live over 100 miles away from my home, BUT, once again, I have made a conscious decision to be an involved part-time Granny Nanny. Once a week I try to go to New York City and babysit for two precious grandsons. I have moved around my career commitments and teach writing classes, act as the account manager for a business, lead writers' workshops and continue my work as a freelance writer on weekends and my three non-babysitting weekdays. A tight schedule, but a rewarding and conscious one. I wouldn't trade it for a week on the beach!-well maybe a week on a beach, but only if I can take my grandsons with me.

My friend Sandy C., a granny-nanny of five from Fort Washington, Pennsylvania, is saving for a family vacation to Disney World. She works part-time and has targeted the year 2006 as the time when she'll have saved enough to treat her grandchildren. She has already alerted her grandchildren of her plans, and the kiddies talk about it often.

But I have learned that I can't make any assumptions about the childcare rules. Assumptions…let's look at that word. To assume—to make an ass out of U and me! How about that! New medical findings, better safety products, and more cautious childcare is a blessing. An important rule for conscious Nanny-Grannies is START FROM SCRATCH about safety rules. Maybe we were lucky, maybe some of us weren't and have tragic memories from our children's early years…the research, the products, the studies about SIDS and auto safety have improved. Follow the new rules! Listen to what the parents' rules are and follow them! Be, not only a conscious Granny-Nanny, but a modern, well-informed Granny-Nanny.

thing. Of course, with two it's a double job. One day I let my two grandsons watch some television, and one pulled something when I wasn't watching and the television broke. My daughter didn't understand how that happened thinking I was able to watch everything they both did. I do my best and keep learning more. It's best when I take each grandson alone."

This is a familiar theme. Grannies and grandchildren blossom when they have one-on-one time together. Shirley K., a Boston Granny says, "I like taking them each alone without their parents. I have a special relationship with each of my grandchildren. I frequently take one alone, not all of them together. I try very hard to handle them individually. I take Evan out on the beach alone for a walk. I send them picture postal cards when I travel, but individual postal cards and packages not a group mailing. I took my 10-year-old grandson to Washington, DC by myself, and I'm taking my granddaughter alone to New York City. They're always lumped together as siblings or cousins so I do a lot with them individually. Even when they all come to my house to visit together, my husband and I divide them up and take them out individually. I'm an hour away from my grandchildren, but I make it a point to see them once or twice a week. Their other grandmother lives near them and doesn't see them. It's more stressful for me when the parents are there too. I do best one-to-one."

Eileen is the co-founder of a web site called igrandparents.com. She has three granddaughters ages 51/2, 2 &1/2 and 5 months. Eileen says that her philosophy is, "I'm here to support my two daughters in the way they choose to raise their children. Not my way but their way. I try to be there for them when I can. My sons-in-law love to be with us. I ask for nothing and give them everything; I put no demands on them. It's their child. Grandmothers offer unconditional love without all the pressure the parents have. We don't have the pressure of having to make all the decisions. I just go along with it. A grandchild is like an extension of my children. For grandchildren…they have more and more people to get love from. The grandchildren feel it…the love. My own grand-mother was just like that. I tell friends; offer to give your daughter or daughter-in-law a day a week so they have a day off and you have a baby day. It's a win/win situation. Whatever they want you do. I have a friend who doesn't agree with the way her children are parenting. I say to her, 'who gets the children all the time, and who doesn't.' I tell my children they're doing a good job. If they ask my opinion, I give my opinion. If not, I keep it to myself. Just be there to support them. That's it in a nutshell."

Individual attention and outings make each grandchild feel special and important. Grannies with whom I spoke all agree that one-on-one grandmothering
brings many rewards both for them and for their grandchildren.

"I'm going away for ten days, and I need a fix fast," says Nancy I., on her way
to pick up her grandson Jake. Nancy is a New York City career Nanny-Granny
with two grandchildren, Jake, age 21 months, and Emma, 4 months old. "Of
course, I'm the premier grandmother. It's very important to me. Jake needs me.
They need me, there's no question about it. My daughter and son-in-law need
me. I take Jake on Thursdays, so it's a definite once a week time. It's so wonderful
for me, for Jake, and for baby Emma and my daughter and her husband."

Grandmothers have so much to offer; you have perspective from having
parented yourselves. You have the experience and you have the specialness that
comes with being "the granny." As Carol says, "I have the luxury of leaving and
going to my own home where it's quiet and where I can have some R&R before I
go back to being 'Granny.' I didn't have that as a mother…"

Stephanie, the mother of Vincent, 21 months, and Kelsey, 4 years old, says,
"We've never had a babysitter. My mother or family members are the only
babysitters we use. My mother is our babysitter 99% of the time. We really don't
trust anybody else. The biggest thing is my mother follows our rules! I trust her. I
know that my mother cares about my children's well being as much as we do. If
it's not us with the kids, she's the next best thing. She loves them. My mother
comes to our house…it's safer and everything is at our house, so she baby-sits at
our house."

Honesty, then, is the key word. Respond honestly to their requests for your
help. There is nothing worse than a grandmother who begrudgingly agrees to
baby-sit and then throws it up in the parents' faces later. Sounds reasonable,
doesn't it? Well, Rose, a grandmother who hasn't yet earned the title of granny-
nanny, can't understand why her daughter doesn't ask her to baby-sit more often.
Rose, however, started out with excuses for why she couldn't baby-sit. Not yet
committed to the role of granny-nanny, Rose often made her daughter feel like
she was imposing on her when she asked for help with caring for her granddaughter. Rose always had excuses or conditions such as preferring a paid babysitter to
be present in case something else came up while the baby was in her care. In time,
her daughter stopped asking for Rose's help. Now that her granddaughter is
older, Rose feels overlooked and her daughter's mother-in-law is the number one
choice to baby-sit.

That doesn't mean that you must always drop everything and be available to
be a true granny-nanny; however, priorities are important. If a scheduled hair-

dresser's appointment has to be changed in order to help care for your grand-child, do it! Your grandchildren are only young once, and later on they might be too busy to fit you into their lives.

Granny-nannies know their grandchildren. They keep up with their activities, growth and interests. If they cannot always be there in person, they pick up the telephone and find out what's going on. The telephone, as you will see, is the best instrument for keeping long-distance granny-nannies active in their grandchildren's lives.

The benefits of being a granny-nanny include: being involved in your children's and grandchildren's lives and their many achievements; providing extended family support, encouragement, and/or companionship; being a better grandmother than perhaps you were a parent, due to years of experience, and continuing the family line. Grand-children also receive important benefits from Granny-nannies like developing positive attitudes toward aging; learning about their family's origins, culture and customs or traditions and developing life skills and leisure-time activities.

If you have made a conscious decision to be a granny-nanny, an active participant in the lives of your grandchildren, you are embarking on a journey filled with responsibility, joy, sharing and meaning. Anything less is your choice.

Your children will feel more secure leaving their children in the care of a granny-nanny, a trusted family member who wants to give something, to leave something and to help her descendants. It is a gift to fulfill this role.

The benefits of being a grandmother are very similar to the famous Helen Keller quote:

"The best and most beautiful things in the world cannot be seen, or even touched; they must be felt with the heart."

3

Twenty Principles For Successful Grandmothering

The principles for successful grandmothering are really quite simple. At first glance they may seem self-evident, but they deserve repeating to remind Granny-Nannies of how best to make an impact and a difference in the lives of their grandchildren and children.

1. **Consciously decide on your grandmother role**. When you become a grandmother, or even earlier, when your daughter or daughter-in-law is pregnant, think about the role you wish to play in the life of your growing family. Do you want to be a once-in-a-while indulgent grandmother? Do you want to be a constant presence in your grandchild's life? Do you want to play a major care-taking role in your grandchild's life? Do you want to be a Granny-Nanny? If you are a career woman, think about how you can make time to be an involved, helpful Granny-Nanny. Plan ahead. Consider your options. When I learned that I was going to be a grandmother I started read-justing my work schedule before the birth of my grandchild. I planned my teaching schedule in the beginning of the workweek, and my writing time on Fridays and weekends. Then I offered Wednesdays and Thursdays as my babysitting days. When my second son and his wife were expecting a baby, I gave notice to my first son and daughter-in-law that I would only be giving them one day a week; and promised my second grandchild the other day. Good planning helped all of us manage our schedules. For two years I have been Granny-Nanny on Wednesdays and Thursdays and fit in my teaching and writing on the other five days.

2. **Set aside special focused time**. When you are babysitting, either at home or at your children's homes, try not to multitask. Give your grandchild your special attention. Don't try to fit in babysitting while you work on some-

thing else like paying your bills. Not that babysitting means sitting and staring at the baby, but it does mean giving your grandchild your attention and focus.

3. **Be consistent as a presence in their lives and as a childcare person**. Grandchildren and parents appreciate being able to rely on you as a primary caretaker. Try to be consistent in your babysitting times. Such consistency helps your children schedule their lives and increases your grandchild's comfort with you. After a while, helping with the raising of your grandchildren becomes second nature to you.

4. **Follow parent rules.** When you are in charge, make sure you follow the parents' rules. Discuss nap times, bed times, diet restrictions, and behavioral expectations with your children so that you can follow their rules. Children thrive on knowing what is expected of them. Don't confuse them by changing the rules just because it suits you better. Respect the parents' rules and they will trust you with their children.

5. **Follow your positive instincts**. When you're not sure how to handle an unexpected situation, such as a prolonged crying period of a young baby, open your arms and comfort your grandchild. Let your positive instinct take over. Check to see if your grandchild is scared, sick, overtired, hungry, or has a soiled diaper. Comfort your grandchild and love him or her. Follow your maternal instinct.

6. **Do not judge**. Withhold your judgments. Give a chance to the parents' opinions on child rearing. They are in charge, even when you are filling in as the primary caretaker. When your son or daughter asks that you not give your grandchild sweets, don't argue or show your disagreement, simply honor their wishes and refrain from offering your grandchild sweet treats. Childcare information is constantly changing, and what worked for you as a mother might not be medically sound today.

7. **When in doubt, leave it out**. This old adage introduced to teach comma usage works well for Granny-Nannies. If you're not sure of something, don't do it. For example, if your children ask you not to turn on the television while the baby is playing in the same room, don't do it. If you're not sure, ask. If you can't reach the parents, and you suspect that they disapprove of

television for their children, keep that TV set turned off. Later on, check it out with them.

8. **Laughter produces more learning than lecturing.** A lot of words are meaningless to a baby or toddler. Your mood, your tone of voice, your smiles and laughter reflect your love and interest in your grandchild. If your grandchild willingly shares a cherished toy with a friend, smile or laugh with pleasure. Even add a few words of praise. But don't see it as an opportunity to lecture about the virtue of sharing.

9. **Cherish your grandchildren's individuality, and don't compare grandchildren to each other.** Cathy, a first-time mother, told me that her husband's mother is always comparing Marlin, Cathy's year-old son, to the other grandchildren. It drives Cathy crazy. Such a warning stayed in my mind, and I make it a point never to say to either of my daughters-in-law that my other grandchild walked earlier or is a better eater. Comparisons come across as criticisms. Enjoy the differences and remember that comparisons breed competition.

10. **Love above all else and unconditionally.** No matter what your grandchildren do or don't do, make sure he or she knows that you love them and will not withhold love if you disapprove of something they do. Focus on the action, not on the child. Never say, "You're a bad boy/girl." For example, say, "I don't like it when you do that. I love you, but hitting hurts me." Your grandchild will learn that you love him or her all the time, even when you don't like a behavior.

11. **Don't drop in to see your grandchildren without permission.** Working parents are busy parents. Even stay-at-home moms cherish the time they have when their spouse is at home to share the joys of parenthood. Call them before you go to see your grandchild. Don't just drop in and risk the rejection you might feel when you are not welcomed with open arms. Respect your children's privacy! Hillary complains that her mother-in-law drops in unannounced at the worst times. "When that doorbell rings my heart drops. So often my mother-in-law comes over to my house uninvited and usually at the worst times. I really resent it. She has no boundaries."

12. **Don't mediate family arguments.** If your child and his or her spouse argue in front of you, don't interfere and offer your opinion. If you do you're set-

ting yourself up to be viewed as a meddler, or as taking sides. If you are present during your child's marital argument, stay out of it! Even if you have an opinion, keep it to yourself. Similarly, if your grandchild is arguing with his or her parent, don't interfere. If you do, one of them will feel ganged up on. During arguments become impartial, or at best invisible. If possible, remove yourself from the conflict to make sure that your facial expressions or body language don't reveal your opinion.

13. **Make memories with your grandchildren**. When you are with your grandchildren take the opportunity to establish a strong bond. Share your interests (if they are age appropriate) and do fun things that will create a lasting positive memory for them. If nature takes its course, your grandchildren will live beyond your life span. How they remember you will be influenced by the time you spend together and the memories you forge in your relationship with them.

14. **Discuss discipline with parents and discipline only when you're in charge**. This is a two-pronged principle. Make sure that you follow the parents' discipline rules, and stay out of it when the parents are disciplining your grandchild. Many modern-day parents use "Time Out" as a way of disciplining their children. Spanking is generally not acceptable. Make sure you find out how your children discipline their offspring and how they would like you to do the same. Then consistently follow their plan. Remember that consistency is very important. Granted, you may tolerate more than the parents would. You are, after all, the doting grandmother. But make sure that you are not undermining their way of teaching their children how to behave.

15. **Set an example**. Children learn best by example. If you want your grandchild to share, you share, be it possessions, food, or taking turns, be a model of the behavior you want to teach your grandchild. A loving, giving granny-nanny helps raise a loving, giving grandchild.

16. **Respect the parents' way of doing things**. Be observant. If you notice that the parents don't stop their child's temper tantrums with food, respect that and don't bribe your grandchildren with candy. Let your children know that you admire the way they are raising their children. Respect your children's parenting skills. Respect them in your heart and with words. My rule of thumb is I don't question the parents' way of doing things unless they specifically ask my opinion. I may talk to my friends about something I disagree

with, but I save my comments about the parents' way of doing things until and unless they ask for my suggestions. Usually a "no ask" means that they don't want to have your input.

17. **Avoid complaints**. Don't constantly complain to your children about their housekeeping, their children, and their rules. No one likes to hear complaints all the time; your complaints bring with them your disapproval. If there is never food in their house for your lunch, bring your own. Busy parents often don't have time or the foresight to stock up on your favorite foods. Remember, having the opportunity to be a granny-nanny is a privilege not an entitlement.

18. **Have fun with your grandchildren**. Enjoy the time you do have with your grandchildren. Make that time fun! Plan ahead. Sometimes it is nice to bring along some new crayons or a new book that you know your grandchild will enjoy reading with you. A granny-nanny learns what things are fun for her grandchildren. Plan to make your babysitting hours a time to have fun.

19. **Baby-sit only when you want and feel up to it**. Children know when you don't feel well or when you are too tired to really be with them. If you are under the weather, try to forewarn your children and make alternate arrangements like bringing a friend along who can help you with some of the more taxing jobs involved like preparing a meal or giving a baby a bath. Supposing you usually take your grandchild for a long walk outside. If you don't feel up to a long walk, leave it out and do something less physically taxing with your grandchild. And, if babysitting becomes a dreaded duty instead of a loving joy, renegotiate your granny-nanny role or schedule.

20. **Make your home safe for your grandchildren**. Make sure that your home is baby-proofed. Cover those electrical sockets. Remove breakables and make sure stairs are gated for the younger grandchildren. Children love to go to grandma's house. They love feeling at home there and knowing where grandma lives. Sandy C., a friend of mine who baby-sits often for her two-year-old grandson, clued me in early about making sure that I have the right equipment at my house. Sandy gave me a discount catalogue on baby equipment that she uses and suggested that I buy a high chair, a crib (of course) and a special box to keep toys. It was the best advice I ever received. Now when a grandchild comes to visit me I have all the right stuff. It makes it more inviting for your children to bring the grandkids to you. One chest of

drawers in the spare room (now called the baby's room) is filled with different size disposable diapers, a change of clothes, and even pacifiers (if your grandchild is used to using one). Luckily, I have the space for this, but with foldable cribs and play mats even a small apartment can house the baby equipment necessary for a grandchild's visit. You owe it to yourself, your children and your grandchildren to make your home child-friendly.

The National SAFE KIDS Campaign offers the following safety tips for grandparents:

- Supervise your grandchildren at all times when they are in your care. Never leave them alone…even for a second…especially in kitchens or bathrooms, around playground equipment, or near water.

- Buckle up your grandchildren correctly every time they ride in your car. Use age-appropriate restraints, including booster seats for children between 40 and 80 pounds. Keep all medications, vitamins and household products in their original containers, locked up and out of sight and reach of children.

- Install and maintain a smoke alarm on every level of your home and near all sleeping areas.

- Set your water thermostat to 120 degrees Fahrenheit or below to prevent scald burns.

- Don't allow children under 10 to cross streets alone.

- Make sure grandchildren always wear safety gear (helmets, pads, etc.) when riding bikes, using scooters, skating and playing sports.

- If there are firearms in the home, store them unloaded and locked up out of the grandchildren's reach.

- Keep poison control center and emergency medical service numbers listed near every telephone in the home. Have a first-aid kit, ipecac syrup and activated charcoal readily available.

- Take a class to become certified in CPR and first aid.

There you have it! Right on, Granny-Nanny. Follow these twenty principles and you will be the penultimate granny-nanny.

4

The Paternal & Maternal Grandmother

Or

Being A Good Mother-In-Law Is A Prerequisite To Being A Granny-Nanny

Is it easier for the maternal grandmother to fill this role of Granny-Nanny than for the paternal grandmother?

According to a November 5, 2002 article entitled, "The Importance of Grandma," by Natalie Angier and published in the New York *Times:*

> *Grandma, what a big and fickle metaphor you can be! For children, the name translates as "the magnificent one with presents in her suitcase who thinks I'm a genius if I put my shoes on the right feet, and who stuffs me with cookies the moment my parents' backs are turned."*
>
> *In news reports, to call a woman "grandmotherly" is shorthand for "kindly, frail, harmless, keeper of the family antimacassars, and operationally past tense."*
>
> *....biologists, evolutionary anthropologists, sociologists and demographers are starting to pay more attention to grandmothers: what they did in the past, whether and how they made a difference to their families' welfare, and what they are up to now...*

The article goes on to emphasize the fact that the greater influence seems to be the maternal grandmother. "It's to be expected that a woman would turn to the person she knows best for help with the children, and that person is much likelier to be her mother than her mother-in-law," said Dr. Martin Kohli, director of the Research Group on Aging and the Life Course at the Free University of Berlin.1

As a paternal grandmother in both cases of my grandsons, I've learned that it all starts with the paternal grandmother's relationship with her daughter-in-law. How to have a good relationship with a daughter-in-law or son-in-law certainly should have been explored before their wedding, BUT it's never too late. If your son loves her and she makes him happy, you should be ecstatic, and the same for your daughter loving him, your son-in-law. What more can we wish for our children!

The maternal grandmother probably has it easier especially since the new mother usually turns to her closest female role model…her own mother. After all, don't forget that the maternal grandmother and her daughter have had many years of practice communicating; however, a good relationship with the son-in-law in this case is vital to the maternal grandmother, too.

Natalie Angier writes:

> *"'And so it is that the maternal lineage has the opportunity to make a difference.'*
>
> *Dr. Kohli said a new French study of contemporary grandparenthood had found, among other things, that paternal grandparents often wanted to do more for their grandchildren, but felt they were not as welcome to visit as were the maternal grandparents."*

Remember, it's not about your ego; it's about being a conscious Granny-Nanny. Here are some hints for bonding with your daughter-in-law, a prerequisite for your grandmothering role if you're the paternal grandmother.

1. **It's not all about your son**. It's also about his wife. When you call or visit, show equal interest.

2. **Your daughter-in-law's parents are not the enemy**. It's not a contest for the most generous, or the most attentive. It's about love and acceptance AND, yes, sharing. Alternate holidays if you prefer not to join the two families.

3. **Don't get in between the young couple**. Anything you have to say, any gripe you may have about your daughter-in-law, don't go running to tell your son. Talk to your daughter-in-law first, or talk to both of them together. Don't try to conquer by division.

4. **Don't compare grandchildren**! The biggest complaint I have heard from young mothers is that the grandmothers compare their baby with their other grandchildren, and the way the other family is raising their children. Stop it! It's as bad as comparing your own children to each other when they were young. It fosters rivalry, resentment, and a desire to shut you up…to put it bluntly.

5. **Communicate directly with the other grandmother, if possible**. Let's say you need to change your babysitting day with your daughter-in-law's mother. Pick up the phone and talk to her. Communicate. You don't have to be best friends, but you DO share a grandchild(ren).

6. **Share photographs**. Let's say you got some great shots of the baby…make extra copies, send copies to your daughter-in-law's mother or daughter-in-law. Carry photos of the grandchildren, your son, AND his wife. They are all your family now.

7. **Stop passing judgment on working mothers**. The biggest complaint I have heard, especially from paternal grandmothers, was about their daughter-in-law going back to work. It's often a necessity, both economically as well as psychologically and professionally. Just because you stayed home with your kids doesn't mean your daughter or daughter-in-law has to. The disapproval, tacit or spoken, is felt by mothers, and such judgments drive a wedge between you and the mother. In fact, empathize with working mothers. Read the book "I don't know how she does it," by Allison Pearson, to get the real facts about working mothers. They don't have it easy, what with guilt, busy schedules, fear of missing out on important childhood milestones, and just plain exhaustion.

8. **Report important incidents to the parents.** You don't have to write everything down (except telephone messages!), but if something unusual or worrisome happens, let the parents know. If the first parent you see is your daughter-in-law, tell her. Don't wait until your son is around, if he's available later.

9. **Get along with any hired help like cleaning services**. Once again, you aren't in charge of everything, just of the baby during your designated nanny time. Cooperate with others working in the household. Ask your daughter-in-law if she has any specific requests for these other service providers, and relay it without judgment to the hired person.

10. **Don't gossip or tells tales when you leave.** As a primary care-taker, you are privy to a lot of things that are none of your business. Keep it confidential. Don't be gossiping about your daughter-in-law or her housekeeping skills, or anything else, for that matter. In this case, if you don't have anything nice to say, don't say anything at all.

11. **Be on time.** Especially working mothers need for you to be on time so that they aren't late for work. Unless something unforeseen happens, be on time and ready to focus on the task at hand.

12. **Leave when you're done.** Often working mothers or fathers come home and want their own time with the children. Unless asked to stay, go home. Don't assume that because you babysat, you can take your time leaving if you're babysitting at your daughter-in-law's house. Working mothers look forward to time alone with the baby or children. The time is precious and not long in some cases, so honor the need for mothers to be alone and leave.

13. **Honor your daughter-in-law's and/or son's privacy**. If you are sitting in their house, don't go snooping. It's dishonest and totally unacceptable. You wouldn't want people snooping around in your house, would you?

14. **Don't assume that having a daughter-in-law means losing your son.** That old saying, "A son is a son 'til he takes a wife; a daughter is a daughter for the rest of her life." It's up to you! I feel as if I have 2 sons, and 3 daughters, my own daughter (childless) and my 2 daughters-in-law, who are like daughters to me.

15. **Clean up after yourself.** Before your job is done, straighten up, do any dirty dishes, and leave things (if you are sitting in the parents' house) as you found them.

16. **Praise your daughter-in-law.** Your wonderful grandchild reflects the love of his or her wonderful parents…including your daughter-in-law. Just the mere fact that your daughter-in-law is trying to juggle work, mothering, wifing, etc. is worthy of praise. Give credit where credit is due. Don't assume that your daughter-in-law is confident, especially about your opinion of her. After all, your son belongs to both of you…so don't be rivals, be family!

17. **Speak up with your daughter-in-law if something is on your mind.** No passive aggression, please! Be honest, assertive, and if something is bothering you about your nanny responsibilities or about your relationship with your daughter-in-law, don't let it fester, talk it out…woman-to-woman. Active listen, when she speaks, and don't blame and shame. Cooperation and love are the keys.

18. **Advance notice.** If your schedule is going to prevent you from babysitting, let your daughter-in-law know in advance. As a working mother, she needs time to make alternative plans. Plan ahead in your own life to avoid unnecessary snafus, but things do happen. When at all possible, schedule other things for times when you haven't made a commitment to babysit. Your granny-nanny services are important both to you and to the parents. Don't take it for granted or forget a promise you made to babysit.

Barbara P., a granny-nanny two days a week, complains that her daughter-in-law quit her job and is a shopper. Barbara's grandchildren are 5 and 2 and ½ years old. She speaks pejoratively about her daughter-in-law's going out shopping whenever Barbara babysits. Even though Barbara claims that she doesn't voice her judgments aloud, I am sure that her daughter-in-law feels her judgment. When I spoke to Barbara I tried to stress the fact that even if her daughter-in-law shops while Barbara babysits, her daughter-in-law may need that time for herself, without her children, and that Barbara benefits from the joys of grandmotherhood, and the time to enjoy her important role. Such judgments do not make for good mother-in-law/daughter-in-law relations. In fact, my guess is that if it were her own daughter, she wouldn't be as judgmental!

Hillary is the mother of a son Jared who is almost two-years-old. Hillary says, "I have my husband's mother and my mother. I just relocated from Phoenix, Arizona, where my mother-in-law lives, and she never saw Jared. She has other priorities. Now I am near my mother, and she sees Jared all the time. She's great!"

Hillary has never been away from her son for a day, but now that she's living in Philadelphia near her own mother, she can trust her mother to baby-sit. "I trust my mother with Jared and with my life," Hillary says. "In the two weeks that I'm back in Philadelphia, Jared has already bonded with my mother. In Phoenix Jared never bonded with my mother-in-law.

"My mother-in-law has no boundaries. She would not even leave the room. when I was in labor and had an internal examination. I asked her to leave, but she just stayed in the room. In my birthing room she was on her laptop computer and tied up the telephone line. A nurse came in and said, 'What's wrong with your telephone. The doctor is trying to call you.' It was my mother-in-law. When they did an emergency C-section, everyone was asked to leave the room. Every-one did, but my mother-in-law stayed put. She has no boundaries."

Many young mothers with whom I spoke complained that their mothers-in-law were very judgmental. Several paternal grannies complained about their daughters-in-law's shopping too much, not keeping a clean enough house, and other petty things.

As THE PATERNAL GRANDMOTHER ask yourself if you would be as judgmental if it was your own daughter, and remember that BEING A GOOD MOTHER-IN-LAW IS A PREREQUISITE TO BEING a successful paternal OR maternal GRANNY-NANNY.

Stephanie's mother-in-law lives far away, but is wonderful with the kids when Stephanie and her husband take the kids to visit them. "We don't leave the kids alone with them when we visit because it's unfamiliar territory, but my mother-in-law is very cooperative. I mentioned the first day we arrived at their summer home in the islands that her glass table with pointed edges was dangerous for the kids. Presto! My mother-in-law took that glass table and stored it in the basement so that I wouldn't have to worry about their safety. She is very considerate and loves the kids."

Sara F., a Granny-Nanny, is the mother of one son and two daughters (and 6 grandchildren). Her daughter Aliya has three daughters, Jalia 5, Jordan 3, and Amil 1 & 1/2 years old. Her son William has a 5 year-old-son Jason and a three year old daughter Jade. Sara said, "There is an absolute difference for all three of my children. It is mainly based on my relationship with my children. For instance, the only ones who sleepover at my house are Aliya's children. She's aggressive about her children having a relationship with me. My son William and his wife keep their kids very close to them. Even my daughter-in-law's mother has very little involvement with their children. Aliya and her husband John are going on a short vacation from a Thursday to Monday. John's mother will be watching the children Thursday and Friday, and I'm going to take them Saturday through Monday. I have plans to take them to see lots of things. It's Aliya and John's first vacation ever. I'm definitely closer to Aliya's children than to the others. It has a lot to do with daughters. It's different with daughters-in-law. I am very careful not to make another woman feel that I have no boundaries. I love my daughter-in-law Beth, but I don't want to step on her toes. With my daughter I don't have to be careful. Who knows you better than your own daughter! My daughter Aliya calls me if the kids are sick and asks me what to do. Not the others. Aliya has made sure that I'm a part of everything. My voice on her telephone was there from the beginning and her daughters knew my voice before they could even talk. I talk to Aliya every day…sometimes a few times every day."

Chrissa is a paternal granny-nanny, caring for her granddaughter long-distance. Her nearby daughter is about to have a daughter. Chrissa says, "My daughter-in-law did ask me if I would be interested in taking my granddaughter, Julia, for four or five days when they go away. I was very flattered, and she doesn't hesitate to correct me when I'm with Julia. But my daughter-in-law Connie sets rules. She said to me, 'You can't ask me to do things, but when I think of things I do them. Don't tell me what you want me to do, but I will do all I can to keep you alive for Julia even though you're long-distance.' Connie likes the fact that Julia loves me. She's very trusting of my ability to care for Julia physically. It's a challenge. We're both very strong willed people, and Connie doesn't put out a lot of personal stuff, and she doesn't engage easily. It's hard to know where she is. A lot of it is I'm the paternal grandmother. It's really around my dynamics with my son, and to make sure I include her. The old rivalry between daughter-in-law and mother-in-law over my son. With my daughter, I'm in love with how her husband treats her. My ex-mother-in-law used to say, 'When a daughter gets married you gain a son; when a son gets married you lose a son.' Sons are more aligned with their wives. The first time my son brought Connie East I wanted to talk to my son alone about something, and that really upset Connie. That seemed to have set the stage. Connie is a wonderful mother. I have very high regard for her mothering skills." So Chrissa can interact more freely with her daughter and looks forward to playing a major granny-nanny role with her daughter's baby, but with her long-distance daughter-in-law she feels that she has to walk a finer line.

Adds Chrissa, "Now that my daughter is about to have a daughter, I'm very excited. It feels closer, and I don't feel that I have to be so careful. I know that if I step over the line she'll assert for what she needs and do it lovingly. It's all mixed in also with the long-distance/nearby factor. My daughter lives nearby, while my son and his family live far from me. My daughter-in-law had everyone in the labor and delivery room when Julia was born in California. If I had been there I'd have been allowed in, but I was far away. With my daughter, I may not be in the delivery room, but she wants me with her before she gives birth when she is in labor."

Carol F. is a 63-year-old grandmother in Florida with two children, a son and a daughter. She has 3 grandsons, her daughter Wendy's 5 and 3 years olds and her son Michael's 17 month old son. Carol said, "I speak to Wendy every day. We've very involved with Wendy's sons. Her oldest has special needs and I do a lot to help her out. My daughter-in-law has a mother who is very involved. My son lives in Connecticut and my daughter lives nearby in Florida, so that's also a factor. With my daughter's sons, I'm the only grandmother. But even if my son and daughter-in-law lived close by I'm not sure I'd be as involved as I am with my daughter's sons. I have a fabulous relationship with my daughter-in-law and she's a full-time working mother with a nanny. My role as grandma is comprehensive because with Wendy's kids my role is as a help and advisor. Even just physically helping her out. She's all over, dragging her one son all over for treatments. My role is that of support. I do a lot with her kids. It's harder with Michael's son because he's far away. When I visit them I do a lot with the baby and I want him to know me. With my daughter, we're extended family. I have had all of them come to my house. My kids have worked out some of their issues together so it's more pleasurable now then in the past to all be together. I'm planning on renting a house for all of us in Martha's Vineyard next summer. My Florida house is child-friendly. There are rules in my house...same as my kids but maybe more freedom. Wendy's house mirrors mine pretty much. I have a crib and I recently redid the babies' room.

"Having grandchildren has absolutely changed my life. At this stage of my life they have added the joy and zest that sometimes felt a little missing. I'm still working but not full-time. But there are times that I'm not available when

Wendy wants me there. I try to be available if she asks but I might not be available. I have my own life but I definitely make Wendy and her sons a priority. I consciously made a decision and I knew before they were born that I would be an involved grandma. My grandchildren are a priority. I think I'm a great mother-in-law, and I have a lot of respect and caring for my daughter-in-law. I'm not a bossy person…I might be more bossy with Wendy because I have that freedom, but I try to fit in with them. My daughter and her husband lived with me for three months with their dog. They still talk about how easy it was. Not one conflict. My daughter-in-law likes me, and she has every reason to. I'm very respectful of my daughter-in-law."

Overwhelmingly, the grandmothers with whom I spoke felt that maternal grandmothers were in a better position as a grandmother than the paternal grandmothers were; this was the theme of most of the paternal grandmothers I interviewed.

Penelope N., a 73 year old maternal and paternal grandmother said, "My son has two children. I love them but I don't have the same connection with them as I do with my daughter Judy's children. My daughter-in-law is very tight about her children. Her message to me is come close but not too close. His daughter Hope is closer to me but his son Jason is 14 and doesn't let anyone get close to him. I never had that problem with my daughter's children. If anything, I see Judy's kids too much. With my son's children I'm very careful. I don't give my opinion with my son, but I do with my daughter. I say something to Judy and I know she won't hate me for it because we're so close. I sometimes can forget that Judy is a grown up. I have a very interactive role with her children. With my son, when I go to visit them I do it their way. and when they come to me I do it their way."

Selma T, an 89 year old grandmother from Washington, DC, has two sons and three grandsons. Selma said, "Most daughters turn to their mothers, not their mothers-in-law, it's a natural thing. Mothers and daughters are close. The best role a paternal grandmother can play is to offer to help but never to interfere."

Anne T., a 64 year old grandmother of two granddaughters and mother of two sons, said her son, daughter-in-law and two granddaughters live about 25 minutes away from her. Anne is a full-time career woman who is struggling with her relationship as the paternal grandmother. She said, "I walk on egg shells with my daughter-in-law so that she won't hate me. I keep my mouth shut. I won't even say anything to my son that sounds critical of his family. They always have overprotected their first child, Laura. Now they have a second daughter and it's different. I see the kids usually once a week either on Saturday or Sunday because they both work full-time and the girls are in day care where my son works from 8AM until 6PM. They build an overprotective shield around Laura, which has made it hard for me to get close to her. But Sarah, the baby is more accessible. They are more casual with Sarah so I have a better chance with her."

Estelle S., an 89-year-old grandmother of five granddaughters and the great-grandmother of five said she spoke with her daughter every day when the girls were little. On the other hand, Anne T., a paternal grandmother said she calls occasionally, and speaks with whoever answers the telephone. This seems to be true in most cases. The contact is more frequent for the maternal grandmother, especially when it comes to talking with their daughters who have children.

The 18 hints for bonding with your daughter-in-law also apply to bonding with your son-in-law. For example, it's not all about your daughter; it's also about her husband, your son-in-law. Show interest in both of them. Stop passing judgment period, whether it be on a son-in-law or daughter-in-law. The important thing is to treat both parents with respect! Good mothers-in-law make good granny-nannies! How well the parents and granny interact has a great influence on whether the relationship with the grandchildren is close or distant.

5

Self-Esteem or Making your Grandchildren Feel Special

All granny-nannies want their grandchildren to grow up with healthy self-esteem. Children with good self-esteem have an easier time in life. They do better in school and, eventually, in jobs. They get along better with other people. They view the world as a place where they are happy and comfortable.

Children with low self-esteem are more likely to have problems in school and in relationships with peers, teachers, parents, and other adults in their lives. They also are more likely to use drugs.

You can not wrap self-esteem in a box, put a bow on it and present it to your grandchildren. Self-confidence and a positive self-image, the elements of self-esteem, are traits they have to develop on their own. But you can help.

According to the American Academy of Pediatrics, children's self-esteem comes from:

- Inborn traits…such as attitude, intelligence, and looks; and,

- What happens around them…how their parents are and the environment they grow up in.

Grandparents can play a major role in nurturing healthy self-esteem in their grandchildren. Remember, it is never too early to start contributing toward your grandchildren's healthy self-esteem.

Sara F., a Granny-Nanny said, "It is important to me to build my grandchildren's self-esteem. Jalia said to me one day that she wanted to be a white girl with smooth skin. She said, 'I don't want my skin!' So her mother (my daughter Aliya) and I talked about it. I try to help them with their self-esteem, but I also wanted to make my daughter Aliya aware of it. Aliya then taught Jalia a song about 'I love the skin I'm in,' and the next time I was with Jalia she said, 'Guess what, Grandma, I don't want to be a white girl anymore. I love the skin I'm in!' I was

31

so happy, and I knew she was building her sense of herself and gaining self-esteem."

The following will help you to do this:

1. **Keep your promises**

   A promise kept will make your grandchild feel loved and important. A broken promise can be very damaging to children's self-esteem, so don't make false promises or promises that you can not keep. Your broken promise may be seen as a message that they don't matter enough for you to follow through. It also means that they should not trust you to be honest with them.

2. **Respect them**

   Your positive words help your grandchildren to feel good about themselves. Call attention to their positive behavior. When you discipline your grandchildren, be careful to show that you disapprove of their behavior, not of them. Be aware not only of what you say to them, but how you say it. Don't belittle your grandchildren or their efforts. Condescending tones, name calling, or negative words or remarks promote self-doubt and hurt children's self-esteem.

3. **Praise them**

   Praise builds self-confidence and self-esteem. Let your grandchildren know that you are proud of them and what they accomplish. Encourage and support the interests and activities that allow them to succeed. Cheer them on. Keep your expectations of your grandchildren realistic, and don't demand perfection. Don't allow your grandchildren to criticize themselves, or their own abilities.

4. **Teach them responsibility**

   Teaching your grandchildren how to take responsibility and do things for themselves will help them feel important, competent, and grown up. Even very young children can help set the dinner table or wash plastic dishes. Older grandchildren can help care for a pet, tend a garden, or complete household tasks. Responsibility helps them feel they are making a contribution and that you trust their ability to get things done.

5. **Let them make decisions**

    As children get older, they want to make more and more decisions. As difficult as it might be, it is important to encourage them to make some decisions for themselves, even if they make the wrong ones. Young grandchildren appreciate the opportunity to choose what they eat for lunch or which video to watch. With older grandchildren, you can discuss the possible consequences of a decision they may make. When they do make a wrong decision…and they will, of course…be supportive and help them learn from their mistakes.

6. **Don't be overprotective**

    Encourage your grandchildren to let go of your apron strings and spread their wings. Encourage them sometimes to take risks. This may be difficult because you want to protect your grandchildren from failure, rejection or being hurt. But, encouraging them to take reasonable risks can help them develop faith in themselves, their judgments and their abilities. Being overprotective can make them overly dependent on you and incapable of trusting that they can function on their own without you or their parents.

7. **Set a positive example**

    Show your grandchildren that you hold yourself and other family members in high esteem. Share personal and family achievements and traditions that everyone in the family can take pride in.

8. **Be a source of unconditional love**

    The best way to increase your grandchildren's self-esteem is to provide constant, unconditional love. Loving your grandchildren will help them feel secure and accepted. Your love makes them feel capable, lovable and smart.

9. **Help your grandchildren accept who they are and how they look**

    Teach your grandchildren to love who they are and how they look…the color of their skin, the color of their eyes, their builds, their talents, their specialness.

Building self-esteem in their grandchildren seemed most important to the African-American Granny-Nannies to whom I spoke. They were keenly aware of the racism and societal "white image" of what is beautiful that their grandchildren would face in the larger community.

Marie A. said, "My grandson is bi-racial; I don't always know what that means for my son who is Black and Ulysses' mother (who is white). I am careful with the books I send and what I say so I don't sound heavy-handed about his African-American roots. His world is pretty white. I'm not just a diversity trainer, but I live it. Ulysses is light skinned but he's definitely bi-racial. He looks bi-racial which pleases me. I'm glad it isn't hidden so people will know right away. He is a child of color, and I try to help him be proud of that. Now my daughter Tanya is dating a white man, but she's clear that if they marry her children will know that they are bi-racial even though she hasn't had children yet. She always says that their dual identities will be clear to her children. She has already told her boyfriend that if they marry she will be talking about Africa, where she has spent time. She, of course, expects that her husband will also talk to their children about his side of the family's roots. Tanya has also already made it clear that I will be intimately involved with her children.. Being a grandmother will be very different with Tanya's children. Her children will grow up proud of their dual heritages and with good self-esteem. That makes me happy. I just want to make sure that Ulysses gets the same thing and feels good about himself and his dual roots."

Children start forming their opinion of themselves and their abilities very early in their lives, even in infancy. When infants cry and find their parents or grandparents are there to comfort them, they begin to feel safe, important, secure and good about themselves. It is never too early to start helping to build your grandchildren's healthy self-esteem. The rewards will be immeasurable.

6

Ten Skills A Granny-Nanny Must Master

Over the past twenty years, increased attention has been given to the importance of grandparenthood. This emphasis on grandparents is a reflection of the increased life span; adults are living longer, and four and five generation families are more common. It is also a reflection of the importance of grandparents to grandchildren. A Granny-Nanny has a chance to be an important figure in her grandchildren's lives. Don't blow the chance. Make sure you have the essential skills to fulfill your important role.

In addition to nurturing and loving, a true Granny-Nanny possesses ten essential skills:

1. **Keep a sense of humor.**

   Child development experts generally break humor into four categories: physical humor, humor of situation, humor involving play or laughter, and humor of character. Children's books often offer numerous situations and a chance to laugh with your grandchild. Sesame Street, puppet play, drawing funny pictures like one of a dog on a bicycle, can be humorous to a child. Children bring the special joy of laughter. You can't believe the importance of humor to children, especially the way it stimulates their imaginations and sense of joy.

2. **Teach by example.**

   One of the best ways to teach children is by setting a good example. Be the best example of a mature, responsible, loving and giving Granny-Nanny…tell them how much you love them as often as you can. "Do as I do" philosophy. If you don't want your grandchild to lie, don't let them hear you lie to someone.

3. **Become a good listener.**

It is very important to listen to your grandchildren to improve your relationship with them and for their self-esteem. Active listening requires love and a real desire to hear what the child has to say, a determination to be helpful, and a genuine ability to accept your grandchild's feelings. A child can be freed of troublesome feelings and a warmer, stronger relationship develops. Give your grandchildren listening time. Good listening is the first important step in talking with children. It means hearing the words and the feelings behind these words. If you listen to your grandchildren, you are taking them seriously.

4. **Talk with your grandchildren.**

Reading, singing and talking with your grandchildren from the time they are infants help prepare them to be successful readers. The sky is the limit. Talk about hopes, dreams, regrets, tell jokes. As important as it is to listen to them, communication is a give and take situation. Don't lecture them, but talk to them and ask them questions about what they like.

5. **Be creative.**

Fancy toys are not necessary. An old box, some ribbons, imaginary games, all stimulate a child's imagination. Eileen says that she plans a lot of creative activities. "I made a 'photo story' book with my granddaughter. We worked on it for three months and gave it as gifts to family members. I make sure the kids have creative gifts for their parents…things they have made with my help." Working on creative projects with your grandchildren can be fun, a learning experience, and a great teaching opportunity.

6. **Be flexible.**

Don't have a rigid agenda of what you want to do on a one-to-one day with your grandchild. Be flexible. If your grandchild is tired, switch your plans to include some quiet down time or a nap. If plans to eat lunch out at a restaurant fall through, be flexible and make a fun lunch together. Rigidity does not work. Things change.

7. **Be consistent.**

Your grandchildren deserve love and some consistency. Providing routine and consistency helps children feel more secure. At times consistency is the most important element in your relationship with your grandchildren. Consistency means follow through. Children feel secure when they are able to predict your reaction to their behavior. Children like to know what to expect. Consistency does not mean rigidity! There is a difference. Consistent love and listening even when there's a change in plans that have been flexibly altered is possible.

8. **Play with your grandchildren.**

Children respond more freely while occupied in playing a game, and problems and fears can often be discussed at these times. Play is particularly important for children. Toys and play provide an excellent medium through which a child can develop his or her creativity, motor skills, intellectual functioning and knowledge about the world. Take time to play with your grandchild for that most important bond between Granny-Nanny and child. Let your grandchild show you how to play with toys. Wait for him or her to suggest a new activity before moving on.

9. **Hugs and kisses mean a lot.**

Genuine affection expresses a Granny-Nanny's love for her grandchild. Hug your grandchildren often. Kiss them when you come and when you leave. Let your grandchildren know how much you love them with expressions of affection. A hug when your grandchild wakes up, when your grandchild is hurt, or for no reason is a meaningful, loving gesture.

10. **Learn to read clues to your grandchild's mood, fears, and discomfort.**

Tune into your grandchild's feelings. Watch facial expressions, body language, and behavior. Often a young child cannot express in words a fear, but if you observe his or her body language or tears you can figure it out. Granny-Nannies learn to instinctually sense when a grandchild is fearful or hurting. Be an understanding Granny-Nanny, one who considers why your grandchild acts as he/she does. Then, act upon the behavior instead of reacting to it.

Master these ten important skills and you will be a successful Granny-Nanny who, from the start of your relationship with your grandchild, will play an important role in your children's and grandchildren's lives. The intergenerational contact reflects a high value for family connection. Grandchildren exposed to such contact grow up less fearful of old age and the elderly. They feel more connected to their families.

7

Nearby and Long-Distance Grandmothers Or "Don't Run With The Scissors!"

Many grandmothers do not live geographically close to their grandchildren. Gloria's daughter and her family live on the Pacific Coast while Gloria resides in Philadelphia. Gloria speaks to her daughter once a week. "The last call," she explains, "typifies the frustrations of relying on telephone calls. I called my daughter," Gloria says, "and in the middle of the conversation my daughter yells, 'Mindy, don't run with the scissors in your hand! I have to hang-up, Mom,' and there is a dial tone." Gloria imagined her six-year-old grandchild Mindy with a scissors in her eye and was on pins and needles until her daughter called her back two hours later.

"Hi, Mom, where were we?" her daughter said.

Gloria, near hysterics said, "What happened, is Mindy okay?"

As it turned out, Mindy avoided an accident, but until Gloria heard otherwise, her imagination had gone wild. This is one of the frustrations of long-distance grand-mothering.

Leslie, whose five grandchildren are scattered between Florida and Georgia, thinks of herself as the other passenger. Whenever she visits one of her daughters she is another passenger in their car and goes wherever they go to see their school, friends and sports events. Leslie's daughter Candy, who lives in Calhoun, Georgia, says, "My mom comes twice a year for two weeks at a time. She knows what my kids do and participates in everything, cheering for Chip at a basketball game, and going to Madeline's swim meet. She follows their sports activities on the Internet. If they are in a special performance she calls and asks how it went. I talk to my mom everyday…with cell phones and the Internet, it's easy. Daily contact is important. My mom positions herself as a part of every activity taking place.

She runs and goes with us when she visits and says she can't understand how I do it…run, run, run. Of course, I remember that she did the same thing."

Candy complains that the other grandmother came to visit and brought her daughter Madeline a doll…and Madeline was 15. "She has no clue!" Candy says. "Some grandmothers come and you have to entertain them, and it's more work than fun. My mom has no agenda when she comes…just to do whatever we are doing."

Leslie adds, "Things Candy and I want to do alone, we do when the kids are in school. I go with no agenda."

The first two years of Madeline's life, Candy and her family lived in Philadelphia near Leslie. Leslie was the 'other mother'…the true Granny-nanny. "Nanu" was what Madeline called her. When Madeline was in the hospital for surgery, the nurse came out of the recovery room and asked the waiting Candy and Leslie, "What's a Nanu?" Leslie said, "I'm the Nanu." Madeline awakened from the anesthesia wanting her "Nanu."

Candy says, "When I had to go back to work, I couldn't have done it without my mother watching Madeline."

Leslie's other daughter Patty, who lives in Tallassee, Florida, says, "When my mother comes to visit it's not a vacation for her. She cooks, shops, cleans, takes care of my kids (two sons Anthony, age 11 & 1/2 and Robert, age 8), and won't even let us pay for our own groceries. She goes food shopping for us. My mom did a cookbook for all 4 of us (Leslie has 4 married daughters). When she comes and cooks and I ask her for the recipe she always says, 'It's in the cookbook. I gave you all of my recipes.' But it's not in the cookbook and I tell her she has to update the cookbook. She's a fabulous cook, and my sons ask her to make all their favorites. My mom follows my sons' schedules when she visits. She takes the boys to Karate and even goes to the school bus stop with them. She comes at least twice a year, sometimes three if there's a special occasion. And we come up in the summertime. My mom is interested in the boys and knows what's going on in between her visits. She knows the boys' favorite foods and favorite television shows. We talk on the telephone everyday."

Clearly Patty and Leslie have as strong a bond as Candy and Leslie. Leslie, in her daughters' eyes, is a true Granny-Nanny.

Patty adds, "If one of my boys loses a tooth, my mom sends them tooth fairy money. If they get an A on their report card, she sends them something."

Leslie said, "I don't want to toot my own horn, but I even know the kids' friends, too."

Patty adds, "The other grandparents live 4 minutes away and haven't seen my kids in six months. When we go to my dad and step-mother's place it's 'Don't touch—don't touch!"…over and over again. It's no fun to go there. If we eat there while we're still at the table eating my step-mother has the dust-buster out and is cleaning under the kids' chairs. Now my mom is different. My boys have a bond with her. Even though we may only see her occasionally, they have a very strong bond."

Long-distance granny-nannies benefit by keeping up with their grandchildren's daily lives and interests. Regular contact through telephone calls, e-mails, and care packages keep the connection solid.

Shirley lives in Boston. Her Albany grandson gets a care package once a month—balls, crayons, books…sometimes even some parent-forbidden candy bar. Shirley's grandson looks forward to his monthly package and feels a special connection with his grandmother.

Rituals can be established with long-distance granny-nannies, be it Christmas together or Sunday morning telephone calls. Grandchildren like routines and feel close to a granny who consistently makes contact. Of course, the most used method of contact is the telephone. Some phoning hints include establishing the best time to call so that it isn't bed or meal time. Ask your grandchildren questions about their lives…things that interest them. And, remember, don't take it personally or act hurt if a grand-child doesn't want to talk to you on the telephone. Send a message of love anyway.

Messages of love through the mail are important. Cute greeting cards, personal letters…not written to the whole family as a group, but a letter to each grandchild separately. Print if your grandchild can read print. Write on a level that meets your grandchild's developmental level. Your grandchild will know you care. Miles melt away when a granny-nanny asks about a birthday party or recital…showing interest as well as knowledge about the child's everyday life.

Granted, the optimum geographic condition exists when granny & grandchildren live within driving distance, yet long-distance grandmas can maintain a close relationship through regular visits, telephone calls, rituals, e-mails and letters.

Telephone calls definitely help keep families connected. The telephone gives you a way to touch base regularly with each member of your clan. Sometime during your grandchild's second year, the phone monologues you've been carrying on will become dialogues…but not the sort that you have with adults or even older children. As a way of showing your happiness with their new skills, you might try building on the little stories they tell by saying something like, "And then what happened?" Two and three-year-olds have their own rules about conversations, too. Their needs and interests come first.

To develop a special close relationship when you are miles apart try exchanging books, music cassette tapes and compact disks. Mail newspaper clippings and photographs. Record special events in audio and/or video.

Another factor in keeping granny-nannies connected to their long-distance grand-children is the attitude of the long-distance parents. Chrissa, a long-distance granny to a granddaughter who is almost two years old, says, "One of the things that comes up for me is that my son and his wife keep me important in baby Julia's life. They have a big photo album with photographs of Julia with each of her grandparents. Julia knows everyone who is long-distance. So she has grown up hearing about me a lot. She calls me Nonny. She sees my photograph and says, 'That's Nonny!' One day when I was on the telephone with Julia I said, 'Julia, let's sing the alphabet song.' I started with 'A, B C, D,' and she came in with, 'E, F, G.' We alternated and sang in turn right through the entire alphabet. For older children the computer is the medium, but for the younger ones it's the telephone. Somehow Julia knows I am important in her life. When I was there (California) visiting and she was 19 months old I arrived at night when she was asleep. The next morning she went nuts when she saw me. I realized then how much she remembered me. It made my day!"

"But," Chrissa continues, "I sometimes feel not in sync with my daughter-in-law. It's important that I have her good will; it is critical to my role with Julia. Connie has actually played a wonderful role in keeping me present in Julia's life even though I live far away. She does it in 3 ways: 1) through photographs; 2) she talks about me a lot, and Julia often says on the telephone, 'I love you Nonny,' and 3) through shared rituals like the Montessori alphabet thing where Connie says A and Julia says, 'Ah...apple.' When they get to the letter N, Julia says the sound and then 'Nonny.' But, I see Julia every two months when I visit, or tops three months. It's remarkable that she still remembers me. If Connie gets pregnant again they're thinking about moving back to the East Coast to be near more help for childcare with family. Who cares why! It would be fabulous!"

Chrissa compares her relationship with Julia with the pending birth of a grand-daughter who will live nearby. "I went with my daughter to buy the baby's going home clothes. I was away when Julia was born. But for this baby, I'm going to take off a week of work and give my daughter and my new granddaughter the second week that they're home to help. My son-in-law will take off from work during her first week home. After a month his mother is coming in to help from Alaska. Three weeks after Julia was born I went to California to help. By the time I came I was very needed. I told my son-in-law's mother that that was a good time, and she is taking my advice."

Patricia W, a 72 year old grandmother of 6, (ranging from 5 years old to 18 years old), and the mother of 4, said that proximity to her grandchildren is the biggest factor. Her younger son David and his wife Susan and their two sons Jonah and Jesse started out by living one block away in Center City Philadelphia. "There's no question about it," said Pat. "I am much more attached to the grand-children who live near me. In the beginning I baby-sat for them once a week, at least. We all called it 'Bubby Day.' I have always spent more time with my sons' children than my daughter's two sons because my daughter lives in Boston and isn't nearby. Then, when David and Susan were moving to a new house, they all lived with us in my house for about two months. We are all very close. When their two sons were in pre-school and moved to their new home about 20 miles from me, I would still have a Bubby Day, and I would pick the boys up at school, give them lunch and spend the day with them. It was wonderful. Now they're older and have friends and activities, so I don't have a regular Bubby Day at the moment. One of the best things we do is once a year we rent a house someplace at Thanksgiving time and my four kids and 6 grandchildren and Bill and I live there from Wednesday to Sunday over the long Thanksgiving Day weekend. We've been doing this for 17 years. We pick a centralized place. It's marvelous. Everyone shares in the cost. We're all adults and we share the cooking. All the grandchildren look forward to it. It's wonderful. This year we're going to the Lichtfield Connecticut Hills to a house with 8 bedrooms and 4 baths on 4 and ½ acres. We also are all together at Passover at my house. These two annual events are very meaningful."

Pat also talked about a milestone in her own life. "My Simchat Chochmah (celebration of wisdom) was a religious celebration for my 70th birthday. The highlight was when all 6 grandchildren walked behind me as I carried the Torah. It's like an adult Bat Mitzvah."

Pat also talked about her role models as a grandmother. "I didn't get a real picture of grandmothering when my children were young. Their paternal grand-mother lived in Florida and my own mother was sick and died when my daughter (first child) was almost 5 years old. My own grandmothers gave me a more posi-tive model. My grandmother would take me alone to Atlantic City with her and it was my only vacation away from home. My other one I called Bubby, and she taught me to knit. She was a definite role model for me."

Especially when there are long-distance grandchildren, Pat emphasized the joy of being away with the grandchildren. "Allison and Cameron, my son Ben's children, would come with us to our summer home in North Carolina. That was always special. But the parents have to be willing to let their children go away without them. Also, it's easier when they're younger. When they grow up they get busy with their friends and activities. I miss the early years when they were younger and less busy."

Pat also learned from her sister-in-law, who had long-distance grandchildren, the positive effect of choosing a children's book and reading the book into a tape recorder and then sending the book and the tape to her grandchild so the child could hear her grandmother's voice and follow along with the tape while turning the book pages. Pat did the same thing.

Loma G. Davies Silcott in her article "Long-Distance Grandparenting: Tips on Staying in Touch" offers these tips for reaching across the miles to your far-away grandchildren.

- Telephone calls are great fun any time of year. If you can arrange to make some of the calls shortly after special events your grandchildren have participated in, e.g. a program at school, you will share the excitement. Ask them to videotape the event and send you a copy.

- Send videotapes of yourself reading a story to your grandchildren. Include a greeting and a short explanation of why the story is special.

- Take pictures of you and your spouse engaged in various activities and send them to your grandchildren.

- Write letters as often as possible and include interesting newspaper and magazine clippings and cartoons.

- Create memories by making holiday decorations and/or gifts for each of your grandchildren.

- Periodically, bake and send them cookies or other treats.

- Knit or sew something for your grandchildren.

- For a faraway grandchild's birthday, buy party hats, favors, balloons and send them to the grandchild to use at his/her party.

- Give your grandchildren mementos from your or their parent's childhood. It might be a long-forgotten favorite toy or book.

- Have your old 88-mm home movies transferred to videotape and give each grandchild a copy. They will enjoy watching their parents growing up.

- Watch a television program together even though you are in different cities. Share your thoughts in letters or telephone calls.

- Have a prearranged time on New Year's Eve for you and your children and grandchildren to each light a candle and make a special wish for the coming year.

- Share your plans and holiday preparations.

- Play checkers or chess by mail.

- Plan visits as often as possible. Visit them or send them travel money so they can visit you.

Jackie M, a 62 year old California paternal Granny-Nanny, said that living near her grandson while the maternal grandparents live all the way in Florida means that she is a very involved grandmother. Her grandson Matthew is 14 months old. She spends the summer at her place in Utah, and it's the longest she has been away from Matthew. She sees Matthew 2 or 3 times a week. Her daughter-in-law Faith has a nanny, but Jackie M. takes her grandson to lunch, goes to their house to see him, and is the major baby-sitter. Jackie M. said, "I have an excellent relationship with Faith. She trusts me completely. I live very close by, and she knows it's easy for me to spend time with Matthew. I'm very close with my son Jeff, which I am sure has a lot to do with it. Faith's working makes it easier. She likes me to be with Matthew. I couldn't be closer to her if she was my own daughter. They've left Matthew with me for three or four days. It's the most unbelievable thing in the world…beyond words. I want to play a big role in his life. I knew that I did when she was pregnant. I hang out with Matthew on the floor, crawl with him or just stare at him. My house is safe when he comes. He is very happy at my house, very good-natured like his mother. To me it's the love or more that I had for my own sons. I watch my son's face watching Matthew and it fills my heart with joy. If we knew how great it was we would have had grandchildren first! I could stop to see him everyday if I could get away with it, but of course I know I can go home and get a little rest afterwards. Being a grandmother hasn't changed my relationship with Jeff because we've always been very close but

Jeff has gotten softer. He now understands the love you can have for a child. Jerry Seinfeld said, 'Now I know how much my parents love me,' when he had his own child. My role is to be another love in Matthew's life. Someone he can always depend on who is just there for him to spoil him a little and give him the time…fun time, a little of everything.

"My mother's mother was very loving. My mother died when I was eleven years old. Maybe that influenced me. I have a need to give a lot of myself to Matthew just as I did with my own sons. Give what I didn't get. The love I feel for my grandson is so intense. I want to be a presence in Matthew's life. I want him to know that he always has my husband Danny and me to come to. I want him to always feel Yay! Grandma is coming and it's a happy time! My husband and I have a busy life. It was hard for me to be away from Matthew this summer for six weeks. I vowed that I wouldn't go away more than ten days at a time except summers in Utah. I know you can't give up your life, and I don't want to. The kids have their own lives. But since Matthew was born I tend to stay home more. Even my sculpting I do less and have taken a little time off to be with Matthew. It's the most fulfilling thing. I had no mother or affection so I have a need to make sure my sons and grandchildren get that. Living close to Matthew has made it possible for me to do all of this. I never stand on ceremony with Faith. If she doesn't return my phone call I call again. Faith says that now she knows what a close family is. I feel very appreciated as a grandmother. They know they can depend on me and they trust me. It might be different if Faith's parents didn't live in Florida and lived nearby. But I live so close to them that I'm a major presence in Matthew's life."

Whether your contribution is large or small to your grandchildren, what you do as a long-distance or nearby Granny-Nanny is important. When a close relationship is formed, this attachment is often developed for life. This attachment comes with the experience of being loved and accepted, a sense of security and warmth, and the gift of a role model grandma, whether you live nearby or far away.

8

The First Time Baby Sleeps-Over

Today, 58 million Americans are grandparents…that's 22 percent of the population, according to the American Demographics and National Institute on Aging. To prepare for their new role, granny-nannies should tour their homes from a child's point of view.

First childproof your home. Comb the floors for small, easily swallowed objects such as coins or paper clips, if you haven't been a tidy housekeeper. Check under sofa and chair cushions for hidden choking hazards. Some more tips are:

- **Know when not to panic**

  In addition to emergency telephone numbers, have basic CPR instructions readily available.

- **Pills can look like candy**

  Don't keep pill bottles handy on nightstands, bathroom sinks or kitchen tables. Improper storage of medication may be deadly to your grandchild.

- **Beware of kitchen hazards**

  Common kitchen dangers include bleach, furniture polish and detergent. Children don't know these liquids are poisonous. Use child-resistant safety latches on drawers and cabinets. To prevent burns, always turn pot handles inward, and use the rear burners. Keep dangling electrical cords out of reach.

- **Make your home their home**

  With a new generation in your family, you and your home will go through many changes. Your own child's bedroom, now possibly your office, will be a nursery again. A file cabinet may be replaced with a crib, but not the same one your children used because most old cribs don't meet current safety standards. The same for high chairs and child-safety seats, which you can rent or borrow, as long they are certified safe. Have diapers, wipes and their favorite toys and foods available.

Now, it's the first time your grandchild has a sleepover at your house. This will begin a glorious process of making your home your grandchild's refuge, treat and favorite place away from home. Prepare ahead of time to help make your home a comfortable, safe place for your grandchild.

After you have safety-proofed your home:

1. **Make sure you have the needed equipment.**

   A list might include diapers, crib and crib sheets, toys, blanket, intercom, baby wipes, a change of clothes, portable stroller, high chair or infant seat, a car seat, baby food, formula, bottles and nipples, bibs and a pacifier.

2. **Find out about your grandchild's bedtime ritual(s).**

   That first sleepover may be scary for your grandchild. To make your grandchild feel safe and at home, find out his or her regular bedtime ritual. Is it lullabies, a book, a cuddle, or a warm bottle?

3. **Start a precedent of familiar toys and stuffed animals at grannies.**

   Buy some toys, stuffed animals, one special blanket and a special book. Each visit your grandchild will see these familiar objects and feel at home.

4. **A comfortable chair (preferably a rocking chair)**

   If there's room, place a comfortable chair in the same room as the crib. If your grandchild awakens in the middle of the night, a good rock while you are sitting will be welcomed.

5. **Get plenty of rest the night before your grandchild's sleepover so that you have energy for your grandchild's early rising, possible middle of the night feedings or comfort time.**

6. **Expect the unexpected.**

   Stay flexible. If necessary, be prepared to sing lullabies and verbally comfort and physically hold a frightened child, unfamiliar with his or her new surroundings.

7. **Plan to make your grandchild's first visit the first of many.**

   Before you know it the toys at your house as well as the crib or bed will feel like your grandchild's special own things waiting at Granny's house.

8. **Keep a night light in the baby's room.**

   If your baby does not need it, you might when you respond to his or her cries in the middle of the night and can't see in the dark.

9. **Respond to your grandchild's fear of separation from his or her parents.**

   A call home may reassure your grandchild when they hear their mommy or daddy's voice.

10. **Call the parents if you have any important questions.**

    This will also reassure the parents that their child is doing fine.

11. **It's all in the attitude.**

    The joy of having your grandchild sleep at your house will be conveyed to your grandchild. After a night of infant feedings and little sleep, don't lose sight of the overall joy of the visit to your house. You can catch up on your rest when the baby goes home and rejuvenate for the next visit.

12. **Purchase a good intercom system.**

    When your grandchild is asleep you can monitor his or her well being with a good intercom system. At night, have it by your bedside and the other end in your grandchild's room, then you will hear your grandchild cry or get up. It is also wonderful at naptime, especially if you are on another floor during the nap period and want to hear how he or she is doing.

9

They're Here! Or A Family Visit

Which brings me to the bigger visits. They're here! You can't wait. You plan and prepare. You end up needing a vacation. Here are some tips that prepare you for the reality and help you make the best of it when they all come for a visit! *Preparation* is the key to successful visits.

Don't impose your ideas on your visitors. Offer suggestions, but let them decide what they want to do. If you have tickets for an event, let them know in advance. It's something special for them to look forward to and will help them plan. Remain flexible, and allow time for just hanging out. That is often the most enjoyable time and provides the best quality interaction.

These tips will help you enjoy your family's visits:

Prepare Yourself:

- Remind yourself that family gatherings may be hectic and take a lot of energy. Get ready by being rested when they arrive.

- Get ready to put your life on hold. Keep your own social plans to a minimum. Notify your friends that you're going to be busy.

- Tie up loose ends so you'll have as much free time as possible.

- If you work and can't take time off, try to arrange a lighter schedule.

- Prepare yourself for the inevitable letdown when they leave. Plan something special to ease your sense of loss when the house is suddenly quiet again.

Prepare Your House:

- Take a tour of your house from the point of view of the ages of your visitors to determine what needs to be put away.

- Childproof your house and put away breakables.

- Keep pills and poisons out of reach.

- Put safety covers on electrical outlets for babies and toddlers.

- Eliminate dangling electric cords.

- Use folding gates to keep the stairs safe.

- Have on hand first-aid materials and baby aspirin, Band-Aids, thermometer, and an ice pack.

- Help your family feel at home by finding out in advance what they need such as crib, high chair, car seat, potty, diapers, wipes.

- Have handy by the phone, emergency numbers of the doctor, the poison-control center, a neighbor.

- Do shopping in advance and have their favorite foods and snacks. Find out what their breakfast routine includes and about special dietary needs.

Prepare for Activities:

- Inquire in advance what they might want to do. Don't assume you know.

- Plan activities for children with crayons, art projects, books, and videos.

- Create a space where they can play and do projects.

- Develop your own permanent collection of toys, books, videos, art materials and games. Children will remember and look forward to them.

- Make sure children have an opportunity for physical activity to burn off energy.

- Build in some alone time for each adult away from the crowd.

- Don't overschedule by making too many plans.

- Remain flexible and ready to change plans, even if you're disappointed.

- Don't promote rivalries by comparing; accept each member of the family for who she or he is.

- Use the visit to demonstrate and teach your culture and heritage.

- If the visit includes some special meals, attempt to prepare as much as you can in advance.

Roll With the Punches:

- Plans get changed.

- Kids get sick.

- Your household will be disrupted, and so will you.

- Your house will get messy.

- Kids don't always sit still through meals.

- Don't criticize your children's parenting.

- Decide to have fun!

Now you're ready! Beds are made. Sleeping arrangements are figured out in advance. Have a snack ready for their arrival since they're bound to be hungry and tired from traveling.

Sandy C's nearby grandson will be christened next week and the whole family is coming in from out of town. Sandy said, "My Texas grandchildren are coming, and the twins are three and Amanda is five. My son Robert and his wife June will have their own room in our house. All three of the kids will be in my daughter's room. I told Amanda I put a cot in the den in case she can't sleep with the twins. She liked that. Friday night all five of my grandchildren and their parents are coming for a big dinner at my house. Saturday morning is the christening, followed by a party at my son and daughter-in-law's house, the parents of the new baby. Then the Texas gang will come back to my house for naps followed by something very special. It will be the first time in a long time that the family is all-together, so I have a professional photographer coming around 4:30 to take photographs of everyone together. I'm very excited, and so are my sons who told me to make sure they get copies of the pictures. My mother-in-law will be there too, so we'll have a record of the four generations together."

Not only is Sandy C. prepared for the big family visit, but also she has made plans to make memories and record the event with professional photographs.

Open your arms, open your heart and enjoy the sense of togetherness!

10

Taking The Baby To A Restaurant

Taking your grandchild of any age to a restaurant can be lots of fun. The earlier and more often, the easier it gets. Starting early will ensure that your grandchild will learn how to behave in a restaurant, and it will become a special treat for both of you. You and the parents should agree ahead of time of certain restaurant behavior, especially for the toddlers like not running around wild inside, learning table manners, and being prepared.

Here are some tips:

- Have some toys that are reserved only for restaurants and make sure they are not noisy and won't disturb the other diners.

- Let your older baby play with ice in an unbreakable cup.

- Put a baby in a high chair just when the food is served…that will help prevent him or her from becoming restless in case there is a long wait after you order.

- Unless you want your grandchild to eat the restaurant's crackers, bring snacks for him or her to eat.

- Feed your baby something before you go to the restaurant, if possible. In that way, he or she will not be cranky and over-hungry when you get there.

- Babies generally make a mess…be sure that you clean up before you leave, and you might want to leave a larger tip than normal for the staff.

- Ask for a table by the window so your grandchild can watch the sights outside.

- Bring along juice and bring a sippy cup or extra bottle.

- If your grandchild becomes disruptive take her or him for a stroll outside, to the restroom or let her or him have some time on your lap. (This is a last resort, because after your lap he or she may not want to go back to the high chair.)

After several visits to restaurants, your grandchild will know what is expected. It is also a good way to help him or her get used to being around strangers. Check out restaurants in the area to learn which ones have baby high chairs or booster seats, which serve food that children enjoy, and which are generally kid-friendly. You want these excursions out for meals to be fun times!

Of course, come prepared for emergencies. That old trusty diaper bag can be filled with teething rings, diapers, baby wipes, bibs, a change of clothes, and a favorite toy or book. Sometimes there is more waiting time than expected and these things will come in handy.

If you have brought another adult with you (a friend or another family member), don't forget your grandchild. Be careful not to get so engrossed in your conversation that you forget your patient grandchild who may be on the verge of tears of boredom. Try to include your grandchild in fun things, new words, new foods and the sights and sounds around you.

You will find that as your grandchild gets older, he or she may ask to return to a favorite restaurant where the memories are warm and the anticipation great. Such a request will attest to the success of your past restaurant visits, and may give you the courage to try some new places. Have fun! Bon appetit!

11

"Grand" Travel

Today granny-nannies live longer, are healthier, and want to be involved in their grandchildren's lives. Traveling with a grandchild is a great way to get to know the child and share ideas, values and stories with them. With careful planning, a trip with a grandchild can provide lifelong happy memories.

- **Parent Permission**

  The first thing is to get the go-ahead from the parents before you even mention the possibility of a trip to your grandchild.

- **What age to start?**

  Chronological age does not always mean a child is ready to travel away from home. Start with a small excursion and overnight. Be flexible. Age four might be the minimum age to take on a trip. Age four through seven have limited attention spans and need lots of hands-on activities like building sandcastles and chasing waves at the beach. Teenagers bore easily so they need their own input into the plans. Ages eight through twelve are the easiest to please. Sightseeing is not a dirty word to them.

- **How many?**

  Taking one grandchild at a time in the easiest option for developing a one-on-one relationship. However, sometimes a sibling or close cousin may provide special companionship for your grandchild. Two children of compatible interests may be a good alternative.

- **Where to go…what to do?**

  Children know what they want to see and do. If their goal is realistic, try to make that the focus of the trip. You do have the last word. Don't attempt an activity that you do not feel up to physically, emotionally or financially.

- **Make careful plans.**

  When you decide on the destination, you and your grandchild can check out books relating to the area. If you live in different parts of the country you can have telephone meetings and set priorities. The planning can be great fun for both of you.

- **Setting limits and making rules.**

  Before you leave, sit down with your grandchild and his parents to outline any rules the child will need to follow. Parents can help you understand what the family rules are and answer important questions. This should be a friendly clarifying talk so everyone knows what to expect during the vacation.

  Some things you need to know include bedtime hour, food or other allergies, medications, special toys or blankets, how much spending money your grandchild will have and whether the child can swim.

  Let your grandchild know that if plans have to be changed, the two of you will make new plans together.

- **How to get there and what to do on the way.**

  If you're going a great distance you may rent a car. Air travel can be exciting but can be tedious. Whether flying or driving take along books, crayons, coloring books, or handheld electronic games to help pass the time.

  If driving, break every couple of hours to allow time to relax, move around and have a snack. Study the map together and have your grandchild help plot the course.

  A key part of the trip is to get to know one another better. The relationships you build now are the groundwork for open communication throughout the years.

- **Be prepared.**

  Take along a cell phone; make sure you have the child's medications. You should also have a copy of the parent's medical insurance card.

- **Pack light.**

  Dark colors don't show the dirt as easily as light colors; underwear can be washed out at night, and mixing and matching is a good plan. Take a semi-dressed up outfit in case you want to go to a special restaurant but other than that casual clothes are more travel-friendly. Neither you nor your grandchild should do a lot of heavy lifting so use suitcases with wheels.

- **Make memories.**

  Take along a journal, stationery and a camera. Keep the camera close by to record things you want to remember. Also, photographs with people in it have more meaning later on than just plain landscapes.

- **You're ready, you're set, now GO.**

  Make sure your grandchild is traveling safely…in the back seat if younger than 12 and in the proper child safety seat or booster seat.

Now is the time to have fun and be flexible. Never feel that any plan is etched in stone. If one thing doesn't work out, there's always something else. After all, a vacation is for spontaneity and fun. You will need patience. Listen and love each other. This vacation can be a precious time. The memories you make will last forever.

12

Helping Your Grandchild Prepare And Accept A New Sibling

If your family is like 80% of American families, then your grandchild will be getting a new sibling. Granny-nannies can help prepare a grandchild for the birth of a new baby sister or brother. With the birth of a sibling, the entire family dynamic will shift. Everybody's role is going to change. It is about more than just welcoming a new addition to the family. It is very important for the first-born to feel that their role in the family is safe and secure.

Make sure the first-born feels as involved as possible in the welcoming process. Communicate with him or her about it. Don't wait until a problem occurs. Even when your daughter or daughter-in-law is pregnant again ask your grandchild how he or she feels about becoming an older sibling. Make sure he or she knows that you care about his feelings, and that they will always be a very important member of the entire family. Begin by letting your grandchild know that he or she will be needed to help with the new baby, and that he or she is about to take on a new role as the older child.

Once the new baby is born there will be more than one child in your child's household. Take turns spending alone time with each child.

Here are some practical tips:

1. Include the first-born in preparing for the new baby's arrival. This will help him or her get used to the idea of having a sibling. Talk about possible baby names, after getting the parents' permission to do so. Have her help plan where the new baby will sleep at Granny-Nanny's house.

2. Do not overlook your first-born grandchild's accomplishments in the midst of the new baby fever. You don't want #1 to feel forgotten.

3. Be available as the granny-nanny for the first born. He or she can have more sleepovers at your house, where he or she can be spoiled a little as an only child once again.

4. Once the new baby arrives, bring little treats for the first-born, which will help boost his or her self-esteem, and reinforce the fact that they are still and always very important to you.

Sara F.'s first granddaughter, Jalia, has a problem sharing her grandmother, especially with her cousins. "Jalia will say to me, 'You're Jason's grandmother too?' She's more acutely aware that I'm the grandmother of all 5 of them, and she doesn't particularly like it."

Dian D. is a Philadelphia Granny-Nanny to her four-year-old grandson Sage. When Sage was born, Dian's daughter Sarah told her that she was going back to work. Dian quickly rearranged her own work schedule, called Anne, the paternal grandmother with whom she's very close, and together they worked out a schedule so that Sage would not need to go into day care. Sage is with Dian on Sundays while Sarah does her food shopping and errands. Mondays and Tuesdays Sage is with Dian through dinner and Wednesdays and Thursdays he is with Anne. Sarah doesn't work on Fridays, so the entire week is covered with family members providing childcare. For four years Dian and Sage have been very close. Dian taught Sage to read, to add, to do crossword puzzles, to play dominoes and other games. Now Sarah and her husband are expecting another son, Cole, and Dian has been actively helping to prepare Sage for his new brother's arrival. Dian talks to Sage a lot about the new baby and about what chores Sage would like to do to help his Mommy. Dian took Sage shopping with Sage's own saved money, and Sage bought a gift for his new brother. Then Sage hid the gift in his closet because he wants to give it to Cole himself. Sage is now sleeping in a bed, so Dian and Sage together washed down Sage's old crib and Sage helped Dian put the crib back together for Cole. With Dian's help, Sage is preparing to be a big brother! Sage is very excited about the idea.

For the early months of the older sibling's life, you have been his or her special granny-nanny. Reassure him or her that you will always be his granny. And that you can love more than one grandchild at a time. Many older siblings feel that they are being displaced or replaced by a new sibling. Be sensitive to these fears and feelings.

13

Divorced Parents—Divorced Grandparents?

Let's start with the divorced grandparent. Often divorced grandparents mean step-grandmothers or step-grandfathers are now part of the family unit. For some granny-nannies this offers a special challenge.

To begin the dilemma, grandma may not like grandpa anymore. Friction may thwart the roles these estranged adults play in their grandchildren's lives. More than one daughter or son with a new baby has complained to me about having to make sure that his or her divorced parents' visits don't overlap, which may mean a dilemma at birthday parties or special occasions. It was hard enough before the grandchildren came, but with the addition of another generation, things get more complicated.

My advice is to establish a genial relationship with your ex before the baby is born. It might mean a telephone call to your ex to congratulate him on the upcoming blessed event. Be the bigger one! You make that telephone call and put the past behind you. A grandchild will tie your lives together, sometimes for the first time in many years. It is important to keep in mind that you will now be sharing a beloved grandchild. Adjusting to being new parents will be trial enough for your children, don't make it more difficult by warning them not to subject you to your ex.

Leslie, a long-distance granny-nanny, says that the most important thing is that people who are divorced should not take it out on their ex. She told me the following story:

"When my first grandchild, Madeline, was born, my ex-husband Ernie and his wife Dotty, my other daughter Patty and I were at the hospital in Altoona, Pennsylvania, while Candy was giving birth. Ernie was so rude and obnoxious to me. His behavior was very upsetting. I said something to his second wife, and she apologized adding that she couldn't do anything with him. It was extremely uncomfortable for my daughters. It was awful. I couldn't make sense out of his behaving so rudely at such a wonderful time.

"Now," Leslie continued, "things haven't changed much. My daughters and grandchildren are older. The infamous brunch is a 'what not to do' story for divorced grandparents. My ex has not yet learned that you should not go visit your children out of town unless you ask them if it works out with their schedules. The night before I left for Calhoun for a ten day visit with Candy and her two children and husband, another one of my daughters told me that my ex-husband would be in Calhoun too, visiting from Florida.

When he heard that I was coming he said to Candy, 'Let her come another time. Let her stay home.' Once Candy reassured him that I would be coming no matter what, he said, 'Well, let her stay home at your house and we'll take you and your kids and husband out for dinner.' Candy refused.

"Finally, I reassured Candy that I would help her and suggested that she hold a brunch at her house for all of us. I didn't care because I thought that this would be an opportunity to make it a pleasant time so that my daughter wouldn't be stressed by our divorce, after all we have been divorced for over 30 years. This seemed nonsensical to me. Ernie and his second wife came for brunch. I said hello to Ernie, and he reluctantly grunted in response. We were all together. His wife answered my pleasantries with one-word answers. It was like I wasn't even there. They wouldn't talk to me. I was the invisible person. No matter how I tried they ignored me. Candy got very upset. When they left Candy said, 'I'm sorry, Mom' and burst into tears. I was fuming. How dare they be so rude in my daughter's house. It was awful. It was terrible for Candy. She has always been the peacemaker in the family. Sometimes you just can't do it. It's a horrible thing. The idea that you could treat the mother of your child the way he treated me is inconceivable. Hate me, but don't do that to our children. The irony is that he is the one who loses, I don't. My grandchildren have no relationship with him, and I do. I'm a true granny-nanny. It was painful and sad. If you treat a parent of your kid poorly that kid will turn around and resent it. Other times in public at a wedding or bat mitzvah it's easier for him to be on one side of the room and me on the other, but in your daughter's house have some manners and consideration."

Other divorced grandmothers told me similar stories. In every case, of course, it wasn't only a rude ex-husband. Phyllis, still resentful of her ex-husband, makes it very difficult for her children and grandchildren by refusing to be in the same room with her ex. What that means is that either her daughter has to schedule two birthday parties for Phyllis's granddaughter or Phyllis misses the occasion. Not a very pleasant solution to a nonsensical prolonged animosity.

Sandy D., an East Coast new granny-nanny of a three-month-old girl (who lives with Sandy D's son and daughter-in-law in San Francisco), has a lot to say about divorced grandparents. "My ex-husband bad-mouths me to my two grown children, but I will not do that. You can not come first when you are a divorced parent. Your kids have to come first. Throughout your life, as long as that ex-spouse is still alive, you want to make yourself look good…you want your kids to like you better…you want to be the greatest. The divorce is never over and you are still married to that other person in a certain way when you share children. My daughter-in-law wanted to know when I was leaving to go home when I came to see the new baby for the first time because my ex and his second wife wanted to plan when they would come. This happened twice. My advice to divorced granny-nannies is shut up about your ex to your children. You have to forgive yourself when you act like an ass. You're only human. It's always hard; it never goes away. You have the right and duty as a parent…a responsibility to be respectful of your kids about their other parent and rise above the jealousies and do what's right for your children. The realization of what divorce really means and the impact of it didn't dawn on me until years later…like at special events like graduations, weddings, the birth of a grandchild. When you see that you have broken up a whole family, not just the two of you, the maybes and what-ifs come in. The first kind words my ex spoke to me after 30 years of being divorced was when this new baby was born and he went to see them alone. His new wife didn't go with him. My son called me and Arthur, my ex, asked to speak to me. I was absolutely floored, and he got on and said, 'Congratulations, Grandma. Isn't this wonderful! It reminds me of when our kids were babies. It's bringing back lots of good memories of when we had babies.' It was the first kind and sentimental thing he had said to me since our divorce."

Perhaps the birth of their shared granddaughter healed something between Sandy D. and her ex-husband. If nothing else, it raised lots of sentimental feelings and memories that may have softened the animosity Arthur felt towards Sandy D.

Sandy D. paused and said, "Your next book should be called "Thirty Years Later" and be about women thirty years after their divorces, especially women who have children. What are their attitudes now about their ex-husbands? How do they share grandchildren? Have they been able to co-parent successfully? That would be a fabulous book!" I will give Sandy D's suggestion consideration.

Sandy D's comments are a reflection of the sentiments of many of the divorced granny-nannies with whom I spoke. The birth of a shared grandchild brings up all kinds of emotions in the divorced grandparents…memories, old resentments, and a sense of still being connected. Depending on the maturity and sensitivity of these grandparents, the birth of a grandchild has the potential of ending old animosities, on the one hand, or, on the other hand, of raising old negative emotions and memories. The true granny-nanny will be able to tap the positive potential of sharing a grandchild with an ex-husband.

"The hardest thing is when long-distance grandchildren come to visit you and you have to share the time with your ex-husband," says Chrissa, after a visit from her son, his wife and baby Julia. "The better the relationship between ex-spouses, the easier it is. When things are good between my ex and me, we share holidays at my house. Now things seem not so good, so my son and his family had to keep moving from my house to my ex-husband's house. My ex is very insular about his time with Julia. He took them to his summerhouse at the seashore and said no one else could come and weren't welcomed. It was very difficult on the visiting kids. Everyone was pulling them in another direction and wanting to be with them"

Sara F. said, "My ex and I have no problem being anywhere together, but his new wife has a problem with it. For the first time in 5 years, my ex, David, spent time with the kids and baby-sat, but it was the first time ever. If we were still married it wouldn't be the case. The kids miss having him as a grandfather in their life. Now my second husband, Antar, is not the grandfather. I've been working with the kids and want them to call him Ba-Ba Antar, which is a term in the Yoruba African language for elder or father. The word Ba-Ba has a lot of respect rather than calling him Mr. Antar. But I don't push for him to be the grandfather, and he does not resent my involvement with my grandkids."

A granny-nanny who is truly committed to being a positive influence on her family's life…specifically on the lives of her children and grandchildren…by very definition must be able to put aside her animosity towards her ex-husband and rejoice in their shared blessings…the grandchildren. Swallow your pride and don't refuse to be in the same room with your ex. Make things easier for your children and grandchildren, not more difficult and stressful.

My ex-husband and I definitely have joy in our shared grandparenthood. I acknowledge any resemblance my grandsons have to my ex-husband, and, in fact, let him know in a positive way. He does the same. We both see grandparenthood as an opportunity to acknowledge our positive feelings about our shared family. Perhaps it is also easier for us since we both have since remarried and have no resentment about not being married to each other any more. Such resentment seems like unfinished business and too petty to hold on to and inflict on our children and their children.

Just remember, if you are divorced and receiving joy from your grandchildren, their very existence was only made possible by the fact of your having had children with your ex-husband. Ruminate on that for a while if you still can't abide to be in the same room with your ex-husband.

It is important to refrain from bad-mouthing your ex to your children or to your grandchildren. Being the child of a divorced couple is difficult enough for new parents; don't add to it by reminding them about how awful your ex is. There is no place for such behavior if you are a true granny-nanny.

Often grandchildren are confused about divorced grandparents. It brings up the fear of their own parents getting divorced, and we all know what that trauma means to a child. If an older grandchild asks you why you and your ex are no longer married, give them a simple answer, not all the gory details of the divorce. Reassure them that divorce does not always happen to couples, and that no matter what the divorced parents both will always love them and their own children (one of their parents).

In some cases, an older grandchild may even be unable to conceive of his or her grandmother and grandfather having ever been married to each other now that their lives are so separate. Don't be surprised by this. Children are very adjustable, and often simply accept a given divorce situation between grandparents as not-a-big-deal. Don't push the issue just because you have a need to present them with all the sordid details. It is not necessary.

Often divorced grandparents bring with them the new spouse, or an extra grandparent. *Voila*…the step-grandparents. A true Granny-Nanny is able to handle the presence of a step-granny or her ex's present wife in her grandchildren's lives. Step-grannies often walk a thin line, and friction between the birth granny and the step-granny should be set aside for the sake of your grandchildren. Your grandchildren know who their mother and/or father's birth parents are. You do not have to feel threatened. Just as you are able to love many people in many ways, so can your grandchildren love you and a step-granny. That is the way it should and must be. Don't ever ask your grandchildren to take sides or to worry about your feelings vis-à-vis your ex's wife's status with your grandchildren.

The following are some tips for divorced grandparents:

- Each grandchild will experience your divorce differently, depending upon their age and their relationship with you. Don't be surprised if they become upset. You are the foundation of the family. Honor the fact that your ex is also a part of your grandchildren's lives.

- Don't bad-mouth your ex-husband.

- If you are dating or have remarried, be cautious about insisting that your grandchildren be close to your new husband or companion.

- Remember that it is not a competition. The more loving people in your grandchild's life, the better for your grandchild.

Then there's the challenge of being a granny-nanny to your grandchildren when their parents (your children) are divorced. Rule number one is DON'T BADMOUTH THE SON-OR DAUGHTER-IN-LAW TO YOUR GRAND-CHILDREN. It is wrong, harmful and detrimental to your grandchildren. They love both of their parents. Don't make them feel disloyal for loving their other parent. It is not healthy for them! Remember, you want the best for your grandchildren.

Often you will be present or even in charge when your ex-child-in-law comes to see your grandchildren or to take them out for a visitation day. Follow the same rules you would follow if he or she were still married to your daughter or son. It is not the time to tell him or her off...especially in front of your grandchildren. Their well being is your first responsibility. You are there to make life easier for everyone, not to poison the air with your negative judgments.

By the way, if you learn that your daughter or son is going to get divorced, never say, "I told you so!" Offer to be a support. Offer your help and love. Divorce is a painful experience under any circumstances, so try to ease the pain. Your son or daughter and your grandchildren will need you more than ever. Be there for them! You might suggest that they see a marriage counselor, but other than suggesting don't start getting hysterical and refusing to accept the situation. Anticipate that all of them...your kids, your grandchildren, even the other set of grandparents...will be saddened by the news of a divorce. Don't add to the problem, be supportive and helpful.

Divorce hurts. It hurts more than just the couple who split up. There is an ever-growing number of grandparents who have 'lost' a beloved grandchild because of a divorce, where the parent with custody 'punishes' the in-laws too. A very unhappy situation which grandparents can find themselves in is if the rift between the couple includes the extended family. An all-familiar scenario may be where grandparents are cut out from grandchildren's lives because a parent...consciously or unconsciously...had found a way of 'punishing' their ex-spouse. The fact is the children will suffer. For a child to cope with a broken family is one thing, and hard enough, but to also lose a set of grandparents as well is to deny a child part of their history.

Be careful about the impact your child's divorce may have on you, the granny-nanny. You might feel rage towards an ex-son-or daughter-in-law who has hurt your child. Even if both partners have contributed to the breakup, blood is thicker than water, and the old protective instinct will kick in. At the same time, acknowledge the grief you may feel at the loss of a son or daughter-in-law because of a divorce. You are a victim of circumstances. The truth is grandparents can be very important for children of divorced or separated parents. Your help will be needed in many ways. The trick is to keep a balance, support your children and their children, but also remember that a grandparent has a special relationship with their children's children...so if circumstances allow it, find time to enjoy just being a grandparent. Your grandchildren will need you more than ever when their parents divorce.

Often the grandparents of a grandchild whose parents are divorced become a port of call for help, and they may be required to be more involved with the care of the children. A 'weekend' parent may find it very helpful to bring the children to your home, and that is where you can help to provide stability for the family that is breaking apart.

Grandparents experience their own emotional pain during divorce and their tentative relationships with the in-laws. They also can serve as models for the careful thought and diplomacy necessary to keep communications open and judgments and frustrations to oneself.

Anne T. said, "I had not seen my ex in ten years, but now with grandchildren we're much better together. We see each other at the kids' birthday parties, family occasions, and it's fine now. I think that having grandchildren healed the bad feelings between us."

A wise granny-nanny will always keep in mind that the 'other' parent should never be criticized in front of the children. However a parent has behaved, to the children they are still 'mommy' or 'daddy' and the grandchildren are dealing with enough without feeling torn by a sense of divided loyalties. Being an active granny-nanny is a task taken on with love. Remember that any divorce becomes a family divorce, and when you see your children in pain, it becomes an unimaginable ache for you. Your grandchildren will feel enough pain, what they need is your optimism and support and, of course, love.

Marie A., a Granny-Nanny to 4-year-old Ulysses, is the parent of Ulysses' father. Ulysses' parents are in the middle of getting a divorce and are separated. Marie said, "Right now I am a long-distance phone call, cheerleader, supporter. I did see Ulysses two weeks ago in California. My son brought him down to San Diego where Harold and I were vacationing, and he spent two days with us at Sea World. He's not old enough for letters or computer correspondence; it's mainly through telephone calls and his father. My son wants joint custody. He picks Ulysses up from school every day until dinner and every other weekend. I have developed a letter writing ritual. I got a loose-leaf book in a binder with plastic sleeves, a box of colored envelopes, and colored paper and stickers. I wrote FOUR on the cover. He has the note book. Every time he gets a letter from me he puts it into one of the plastic sleeves. Every two weeks or so I send him a letter. At the end of the year he'll have 20 or 24 he can look at. Next year I'll get one that says 5. Later he'll send me things so I will have a binder that says Ulysses. I definitely want to be a presence in his life. When I saw him after one year he knew who I was and wanted to sit with me and hold my hand. He seemed very comfortable with me. He remembers a lot from my last trip to see him. When I call I remind him of things we had done together so that I stay in his mind. At the end of a phone call I say, 'Who loves you?' and he says, 'You do.' We have established rituals for a lifetime. I had a relationship with my daughter-in-law, but as things changed between my son and her, it changed between us. So I talk to her occasionally at holidays. My son encourages me to include her but I stopped because she wasn't interested. I also suspect she was using me and my relationship with my son in ways that were unhealthy. She has rules for my son and probably will have them for me too. Eventually, I think my grandson will make sure that he has a relationship with me. I think it's important to have a relationship with your grandchild because the relationship between the parents is ever changing, and the only continuous relationship I can count on is the one I try to make happen with my grandbaby. So my relationship with him doesn't rely on their relationship as parents. It's a real commitment, and I just can't have a whim and fly out to see him. It has to be scheduled. There's a commitment not to surprise each other. It's challenging…even though I'm establishing my own relationship with Ulysses, he's still only 4 so I need help. My son has to be my cheerleader.

"For instance, my son called and said Ulysses said he wanted to talk to Grandma Rie (that's what he calls me). Ulysses initiated the call but someone had to make that call, and my son did. My son lets me know what Ulysses is into. I don't always get a lot of feedback about things I send for Ulysses. I sent him Spi-der Man because my son told me Ulysses loved Spider Man. It was a big hit.

"My ex-daughter-in-law is Italian and lots of times she turns to her parents. Holiday time honors the Italian tradition, not our African-American roots. My son has to be the one. I have to learn to keep my thoughts to myself. Ulysses is a child of color, and I want him to know that and be proud of that."

Tips for Maintaining Your Relationship with Your Divorced In-Law Kids

1. Reach out to your in-law child and state your intentions to stay in your grandchildren's lives.

2. Let him/her know that you want to remain involved with the grandchildren.

3. State your desire to continue to have family celebrations.

4. Indicate that you'd like to help out (give specific suggestions).

5. Express your sympathy for the situation.

6. Don't place criticism and blame.

7. Avoid getting in the middle.

8. Don't burden them with your own feelings.

9. Display your good will.

The in-law grandparents also require thought. Even if you are not very close it helps to give them the courtesy of a call or note to acknowledge the divorce and the change in the family. It is easier for the grandchildren when the two sides remain friendly. On the other hand, if you have a relationship with the other grandparents, reach out to them. It may be awkward but, unfortunately, divorce creates many awkward situations. Remember, in divorce, the grandparents are often the forgotten casualties.

Life can get more complicated when either the grandparents or parents are divorced, but your job as granny-nanny is to be supportive, loving, and under-standing. Put aside your animosity towards your ex-husband. Put aside your anger at your son-or daughter-in-law. Reassure all of them that you will adjust to the new situation. If asked your opinion, you may give it, of course, as long as it is sound and does not add to an already tense situation. Encourage your child to acknowledge the importance of both children and grandchildren to be able to maintain a good relationship with both sides of a divorced couple. Just because the parents or grandparents are divorced doesn't mean that a parent is also divorced from his or her own child. That precious parent-child relationship is forever…and for better or worse.

Many children suffer from the belief that they have caused their parents' divorce. Granny-Nanny can reassure them that they are not responsible for the break-up and should not place guilt on anyone. Many Granny-Nannies are the saving grace in a child's life during a period of tension. Children don't do well when they feel the hostilities of two persons whom they love but who have ceased to love one another. Here Granny-Nanny can provide a steadying world of warmth. They will like having a safe place in the world they can always come to, and that their Granny-Nanny won't desert them and is "on their side."

Reassure your grandchildren. Let them know that they are loved by their parents and grandparents, divorced or not. Grandchildren should not be forced to take sides.

14

Step-Granny-Nannies

Gone is the day when Grandma is a soft, gray-haired lady who stays home and bakes cookies. Many Granny-Nannies take an outside job to fulfill themselves or to earn extra money. Maybe the kids have moved halfway across the country to follow their own dream. Enter a new phenomenon: Up to 33 percent of persons 65 years and older are step-grandparents.

As people move in and out of relationships, more and more children find themselves in a step-situation. This sometimes involves stepparents as well as half or stepsiblings. Each of these entities comes complete with an extended family.

What is a granny-nanny's role in this new and changing family structure? Along with the stresses of trying to be a conscious Granny-Nanny today come the complexities of a blended family. The addition of a step-grandparent sometimes means a lack of history in the relationship. If you are a step-Granny-Nanny how can you be an effective grandparent?

Time. Time spent with the child, the natural passage of time. Love and respect take time, even from birth. Make a point of spending quality, one-on-one time with a step-grandchild. Talk to him or her, ask questions, listen, watch, and take an avid interest. Go beyond your limits and stretch. Give him a chance to know who you are and figure out his place in your life. If you are met with resistance, gently persist.

Recognize Differences Without Being Different

If you are a new addition to an already established family, you may have to struggle to be a part of your step-grandchild's life. If you have other grandchildren to whom you are their granny-nanny and not a step-granny-nanny, your step-grandchild knows the difference. Equal, Equal, Equal. There can be no difference made ever. Not in gifts, attention, behavior, nothing. Take into consideration personal taste and personality. All kids are different, unique individuals. Don't give a step-grandson a basketball as a gift if you know he prefers to read just because your other grandson is getting a basketball. Conversely, don't give him a book if your "real" grandchild is getting a bicycle. Every effort has to be made not to make your step-grandchild feel like a lesser person than the natural grandchild. In all ways, at all times, equal. Favoritism has no place.

I'm Okay, You're Okay, but She's…

The acceptance of a remarriage will have a strong affect on the relationship with a step-grandchild. Learn to know the child, learn to love the child for who she is.

Those "Other" People

A natural grandchild usually comes after two families have gotten to know one another; their children have decided to make a life together. But a step-grand-child comes with an entire set of "other" grandparents that you may never meet. A word of warning: this extended family is a part of your new grandchild and he will keenly feel any hint of criticism. If you want to build a relationship worthy of being called granny-nanny, resist all temptation to bad-mouth the "other" grand-mother.

Step-grand parenting can be the most rewarding job you'll ever have. You can be a force in a young person's life that makes a difference for a lifetime.

Some guidelines for step-granny-nannies:

- Try to educate yourself about stepfamilies.

- Know each stepchild as an individual.

- Give everybody time.

- Be sensitive to your stepchild's change of status.

- Try to have a special place for your step grandchild's things at your home.

- Respect your step grandchild.

- Be flexible about your differences. Use humor and avoid quid pro quo (tit-for-tat)

- Be your self.

Judi E., a Philadelphian, has no birth children of her own. Her husband Perry, however, has two children. Perry's daughter has a four-year-old daughter named Marlee. Judi E said, "Marlee has brought so much joy and amazement to my life. I see her once or twice a week, and she comes by herself to our seashore house. She tests her femininity through me. We do manicures and play beauty parlor. Her father's mother lives in Florida. So I'm it! Marlee is a cuddler. She is a gift that I never expected to have since I don't have any of my own children. To be in a position to really impact Marlee's life is a gift to me. It's not a patchwork quilt but you have to be there, an intricate part of their lives. A grandma can look at a grandchild differently than anyone else can. It's about the child's self-worth and value. There's something profound in a grandma's look. I consider myself Marlee's grandma, and she considers me her Mom-Mom, her special grandparent who loves her very much. Marlee does not know about step this or step that, I'm just her grandmother."

And that's the way it can be. You can make it work!

15

Gay Granny-Nanny

We not only have Granny-Nannies who are "heterosexual," but we have lesbian Granny-Nannies too. Some are activists, some are closeted, and some may never get to see their grandchildren.

Victor said his marriage fell apart over his wife's discomfort with her lesbian in-laws. Victor's wife demanded that there be no contact between their baby daughter and her gay grandmother. This opened Victor's eyes up to the prejudice his mother faced. Victor said, "I don't look at people for their sexual orientation. My mom's lifestyle is her lifestyle. You have to respect that." As for his mother's partner and his step-siblings, Victor said, "I consider them family now. I'd do anything for them. My mom is not my gay mom. She's my mom and the grandmother of my daughter."

Two lesbian granny-nannies with whom I spoke call themselves "The Bubbies," a Yiddish term for grandmother. Carole S., one of the Bubbies, has two children from her past marriage and two grandchildren, a 7-year-old granddaughter and a 3-year-old grandson. She is also Bubby to her partner Marge's two chosen grandchildren.

Carole said, "When I was a little girl my Bubby was my hero up until the day she died. She'd say, 'Carole, I look at you and I qvell.' Now I get it! I work for the Head Start program for the school district of Philadelphia for 5000 kids. My oldest son is married to a fundamentalist family. I promised them I wouldn't talk about my life style with my daughter-in-law's parents. My future son-in-law—-I told him I will not make the same promise I made to my daughter-in-law. I'm comfortable with who I am, and I won't hide it. I'm out at work, and I'm not going to hide.

"I did not have a very happy childhood. My mother wasn't very nurturing. My grandmother was the light at the end of the tunnel. When I struggled with my sexual identity I went to my grandmother who said, 'Go marry, you'll be fine.' I did do that because I wanted children. I have a son Benjamin who is 36.

During the next 4 years after I married I realized I wasn't happy, but I didn't want my son to be an only child so I had twins. My marriage ended when the twins were 2 and ½. I was in a 15-year relationship with a woman. She died. Now my partner and I have been together for 13 years. My oldest son went to college, and during his third week of school he fell in love. He got married and has two children. Her family were fundamentalist Christians. It was bad enough that my son is Jewish but how about me—a gay mother. I am straight around my daughter-in-law's parents. My partner and I are very involved with my grandchildren and baby-sit all the time. I'm Bubby and she's Bubby Marge. We haven't yet talked with my son and his wife about what to tell my 7 years old granddaughter when she asks about my relationship with Marge.

"But—no matter—our home is the center. We have the family Chanukah party. For my granddaughter Katlin I had her first birthday party at my house. My ex-husband's sister and her husband came. Hey, we're grandparents, so the first three years I invited my ex-husband and his wife. We get along great. My daughter is getting married, and my ex-husband and I are walking her down the aisle.

"My son Benjamin lives in York, Pennsylvania, which is 2-2 and 1/2 hours away. We talk all the time, and Katlin has email so we communicate. She asked me to teach her how to knit. I went and stayed overnight to start to teach her. Being a Bubby is the best thing in the world. It doesn't get any better than grandkids. Now I get it! It doesn't matter if they are my biological or chosen grandchildren, there's something very special about grandkids.

"I see my role as historian, and a place they can come and be whatever they want to be. Katlin and I drove to New Jersey to meet my daughter and to get her marriage license. We took the Benjamin Frankin Bridge. I told Katlin the story about when her Daddy was little he thought it was his bridge. That's part of his history and it's fun to pass that on. She liked that story, and later when we came back over the bridge she said, 'We're going over Daddy's bridge.' Because my grandchildren are in interfaith families, I see part of my responsibility is to make sure the kids know about their Jewish heritage. I make sure we have Passover Seders, Chanukah celebrations. I'm pretty open to do whatever my grandkids want to do. For me, it was always safe and special to be at my Bubby's. I want to replicate that. I will keep you safe, is the message I want to convey. I'm my grandchildren's link to the past and they are the future. Hopefully, they will get to know me as a person before they know me as a gay person. Hopefully that will help make them be more accepting of all kinds of people. Children aren't born hating.

We teach them that. We have a responsibility to teach them acceptance. Knowing us first as grandparents and then as gay women will help.

"Katlin said, 'Poppy is Ben's daddy and you and Poppy don't live together anymore, but you live with Bubby Marge now.' And I said, 'Yeah, I do.' Kids don't keep secrets.

"My future son-in-law is from Alabama. My daughter told him almost immediately that her mother was a lesbian. When I knew that they were serious about each other I told him that the promise I made to stay in the closet with my daughter-in-law's family I wouldn't make with his family. He called his mother the next morning and told her everything—about my being a lesbian, and they were fine. We've met them. We went to Alabama for a shower, and then to North Carolina to meet his parents. They seemed very accepting of our life style, and it seemed to give them license to talk about their life more openly.

"Our home is child-friendly. We keep toys and books here. This is the Bubbies' house. It's a very kid-friendly house because we're kid friendly. We don't buy things for the kids every time we see them. We are the gifts. I'm the gift. Do with me what you will. You can dress me up and do crazy things with me. I never wanted it to be, 'Bubby's here, what did you bring me?'

"I have big shoes to fill. My bubby was a very special lady. She had cerebral palsy yet she raised four kids and me and worked too. She never let her cerebral palsy interfere with anything she wanted to do. She was the little beacon in my childhood. I think it's important to be open but respect the parents that your children are. I know I raised my son to be the best person he could be. He's a great Dad and a wonderful husband, and I respect that. I wouldn't be open about my life style with my grandchildren without having a discussion with my children first. My grandchildren are not my children. It's important to remember that our children are the parents, and if we raised them right they will make good decisions."

Carole went on, "I came out when Benjamin was 6 years old and the twins were two. At Benjamin's Bar Mitzvah I thought it was time to tell them. When I did they said they already knew. When my first partner died, Benjamin and the twins lost a parent and they sat Shiva for her. My daughter was closer to her than she was to me. She wants to honor her at her upcoming wedding, and she accepts Marge, but it took a while like with any couple when one dies. Marge never pushed herself, and she let them find their way to her. Now they have an awful lot of love and respect for her. My twins often are at odds with each other and call Marge Switzerland—the place to go where there are no sides."

Carole was one of the most joyful granny-nannies I interviewed. She kept repeating, "Being a grandma is the best thing in the world. Those of us who get to be grandparents are very lucky people. I became a chosen Bubby at 49 and a biological Bubby at 50. Biological or chosen, it doesn't matter. I changed careers in my 40s and went back to nursing school at 47. The day Katlin was born I had to take a final examination in pharmacology. At 4AM Benjamin called to say they were on the way to the hospital. I took the exam and then ran to the hospital and saw Katlin when she was about an hour old. There are no words to describe the feeling when you look at a baby that you know is a part of your child. When I looked at Katlin and my son Benjamin holding her, that vision—my son holding his baby—there are no words! Here's the person I gave life to holding a life he created. It's absolutely magical!"

Talking with Carole was absolutely magical for me, and became even more magical when I interviewed her partner Marge, the other half of The Bubbies.

Maggie's children Jonah 8 and McKenna 5 are Marge's chosen grandchildren. Maggie is the daughter of the man Marge went to her senior prom with. Maggie came out to Marge when she was sixteen. Her father who died 2 years ago raised her. In many ways, Marge was there as Maggie's chosen mother since Maggie's biological mother has been institutionalized for many years. "I was the one who took Maggie for her first bra. Maggie and her partner Donna moved to Philadelphia because Carole and I are here," Marge explained. "When Jonah was born I made a conscious decision that I was going to be involved. At first it surprised everyone, especially Donna. I wanted to be there for Maggie because she didn't really have anybody. Carole and I were the cheering section the whole time. Plus we were local and here. We were here for it all and became instant grandmothers. It just evolved.

"My role with the kids is to teach them things their parents won't. Dirt and water things. I like to be the person who sits quietly with them and just lets them talk. I sit on the porch swing with all of them. Jonah is aware that I'm gay and also that his moms are. It's easier for us that his moms are gay too. McKenna is a tough little girl with well-formed opinions. She is going to be the flower girl with Katlin at Carole's daughter's wedding. Jonah will be a ring bearer. McKenna put her foot down about why girls have to do flowers and boys rings and said she'd like to have the ring job. She tried on the dress and shoes for the wedding and she likes dressing up. She is very fashion conscious and things must match. Imagine two lesbians having a girlie-girl.

"We are The Bubbies—a match set. To Benjamin's kids we're Bubby and Bubby Marge. I would like the four of them to be together more often but it doesn't seem to work out that way all the time. We have more of a family feeling because of the grandchildren. We get to be proud of them together. I want to protect them from the bumps that will happen if they get gay-bashed, especially about their mothers. Maggie and Donna consciously choose multi-cultural books, music and different kinds of families type stories. I've not seen that at Ben's, especially in terms of gay families, though they do have multicultural toys. Carole and I—the two of us have a wonderful family together."

Clearly, gay granny-nannies feel the same special feelings about their grandchildren as all granny-nannies; however, they do anticipate the possibility of the grandchildren having questions about their gay-grandparents' life choices.

Not all of the gay grandmothers with whom I spoke had such accepting families. Joan C., the mother of five sons and 6 grandchildren, lives in Cape May, New Jersey. Joan said, "I don't play a role in all of my grandchildren's lives, but do with my 3 year old and 1 year old grandchildren, the children of my son in Boston. I have two in Florida, but my Florida son won't allow me to have a relationship with his children. But I send the Florida grandchildren cards and gifts and talk to their mother every two months to see how they're doing. My youngest and oldest sons have a relationship with me, but the other 3 sons refuse to have a relationship with me due to my divorce and my life choice as a lesbian. My partner Annie and I live together in New Jersey. Unfortunately, however, we have a fractured family because of 3 of my sons who don't approve of the choices I've made. It's very painful for me. I have tried repeatedly to have some healing with these sons, but to no avail. I have tried. As for nearby and long-distance grandchildren, my granddaughter lives nearby but my son won't let me see her. I did see her until she was two years old, but only alone. I wasn't allowed to bring my partner. I'd see her once every six weeks. But, after my ex-husband died it got worse, and he didn't want me involved at all. My son in New York is the most alienated from me, and I've never seen his daughter—my granddaughter. I think I feel worse about the fact that this gets passed from generation to generation—the bitterness. Hopefully, one day it may change. You can only control what you can control. Every day I hope that something will happen and the alienated ones will feel differently. Maybe after I'm not here any more they will know a little bit about me and know that I care.

"No matter how, you can figure out a way that you can leave a legacy. I think that's important. We all can't do it in the way we'd like to. It's important for my grandchildren to know that I love each and every one of them even if I couldn't see them. I keep a journal for each of them—a separate journal for each. It will be about who I was and a sense of me and the life I led and my feelings for them."

Joan's divorce and relationship with her ex-husband did have a strong influence on her relationship with her sons and grandchildren. "My ex-husband's attitude," Joan explained, "was so important. My ex felt betrayed and was very bitter and he wanted his sons to feel the same way so they had to choose—split loyalty. My ex-husband felt victimized by me and my sons who are alienated felt they should be loyal to him. It depends on how the couple works it out and if they go on with their lives. It's a lot about divorce. My being gay was a perfect excuse for my ex-husband to put all his venom on. His cry was he was wonderful and he had no choice—your mother chose a woman."

Joan's alienation from 3 of her sons and their children is very painful for her. She said, "It's a shame. It destroys people and they don't seem to see the implications for generations to come."

After speaking with Carole, Marge and Joan it became very clear that the kind of granny-nanny a gay grandmother might be is strongly affected by the relationship not only with the gay grandmother's children, but also with her ex-husband. Both divorce and parent/child relationships have a stronger impact on the granny-nanny's relationship with her grandchildren than geographic proximity.

On the subject of Granny-Nannies whose child is gay and has children, either adopted or through insemination, some mention should be made. Those Granny-Nannies with whom I spoke were active in their grandchildren's lives and made no distinction between those grandchildren and biological grandchildren. Mary Ann B. was typical of those super Granny-Nannies.

Mary Ann B. said, "There is no difference between my biological daughter and son-in-law's two sons and my gay son and his partner's adopted daughter and son, as far as my role as Mom-Mom (the name her grandchildren call her). I see my son's 4-year-old son and 2-year-old daughter at least twice a week. When my son and his partner adopted their son my husband went with them in the delivery room. I play a key role in all my grandchildren's lives. I pick up Scott twice a week and spend the day with him. I was helpful I think when Scott became a big brother and I stayed with him when my son and his partner went to get their new daughter. One day my son took his daughter shopping and the saleswoman said to her, 'Where's your Mommy?' She answered, 'No Mommy, two Daddies.' The woman was taken aback at first. When I read stories to her and there's a mom and dad in the story I sometimes say Daddy and Mom-Mom. The kids' school is very accepting too. The kids have a wonderful family life. My husband and I are older now than when my daughter's sons were born. Her sons are 15 and 16 now. We have more time to spend with the little ones, and we want to, not out of obligation. We keep toys at our house and they come over to play. They go to a small private school. When my son and his partner went for the acceptance interview they asked me to come with them, especially since I was an early childhood teacher for many years, and they valued my opinion. I did go with them, and when it was over I said I would definitely send the kids there. It was a wonderful school. My daughter used to call me all the time when her sons were little and now my son calls me for the same sorts of things. There is no difference. I'm the one who shortens the kids' pants and I'm the back up person for gymnastics and visits to the pediatrician. There is no line drawn. I think it is because I have a good relationship with my daughter and her husband and with my gay son and his partner. That makes the difference."

The Granny-Nannies of grandchildren being raised by gay parents seemed no different than the Granny-Nannies of heterosexual children. They view their grandchildren as equal to their biological grandchildren, and play the same active role in both of their lives.

Gay Granny-Nannies face the biggest challenge—how to be authentic, loving grandmothers while living authentic loving lives of their own. The obstacles are many from societal to familial roadblocks and homophobia. The message they want to send to their grandchildren is the same as the message that heterosexual granny-nannies want to send; that is, unconditional love for their grandchildren. The same message granny-nannies of grandchildren whose parents are gay also want to send!

16

Chosen Granny-Nanny

There is a special category of Granny-Nannies—that is the Chosen Granny-Nanny, a woman who isn't the grandmother by birth or in-law relationship, but someone the parents or even the children carefully choose to fill that role. Judi E. explains her role as a chosen Granny-Nanny quite well.

Judi E. said, "When Ron and his wife became pregnant, they sat with my husband Perry and me and said that they'd like us to be the real grandparents. Ron's mother was my first cousin, and she died very young. Ron is my Godson. Ron's wife Mindy's mother was also not alive. It was very emotional for me since I have never had children of my own. Ron is my only intimate, immediate blood relative—and this gift of a grandson with my blood awed me. I have lost my whole family. Andrew, my grandson is very special to me. He's something I thank God for every day of my life. My relationship with my grandson Andrew is amazing. I see him every week. Now Ron and his wife Mindy are divorced, and Mindy has remarried, but I am still the grandma. I have worked hard to maintain a good relationship with Mindy, too. I include Mindy with Andrew when he's with her (Ron and Mindy have joint custody). That way Andrew doesn't feel that the family is separate. Andrew has taught me, a motherless woman, so much. He's given me such joy. Apart from the blood connection, Andrew and I are connected for life. Just about everything I know about spontaneity I have learned from Andrew. As a career woman, I did things only after careful planning. Andrew has taught me through his love how to be spontaneous, how to do things without planning it out first. He taught me through his love about being confident even when I am not wearing my usual make-up. The gift of just being okay with me in a non-career role is something I learned from him. Being a Granny-Nanny isn't about planning everything or making a perfect dinner. It is about being fully present now! What's important to them is that you are able to be fully present with them. It's more important than their thinking that Grandma makes a good chicken soup. I've been humbled and graced by Andrew. I can't imagine feeling different if he was born of my own child. Andrew will be seven soon. For the past seven years he has enriched my life, and I like to think that I have enriched his life, too. It's imperative to understand that this is about the kids not about you. Shame on you if you let anything get in the way of your relationship with a grandchild. You need focus and perspective."

On discipline and following the parents' rules, Judi E. said, "I see grandmothering as a chance for kids to test the limits and within certain boundaries abandon the rules. I see grandmothers as the teachers of values rather than as the teachers of discipline. My house is a place where Andrew learns that he can break rules and still be okay and loved. I go everywhere for Andrew—visiting day at his school, his school plays. I said to Mindy the other day, 'Andrew is perfect!' Mindy answered, 'Spoken like a true Grandma.' That meant a lot to me."

Judi E. also has a step granddaughter, Marlee, who is four years old. "Marlee and Andrew are close. Andrew told me the other day that he wanted to come to my house without either of his parents. Andrew always refers to me as 'my grandmom'—not Grandmom but MY grandmom. It feels to me like this is the embodiment of my being his Granny-Nanny. What is important is to be part of the fabric of Andrew's life. Grandchildren and grandmothers need to be connected, not just someone that you have dinner with once a week. Andrew calls me My Grandmom and Marlee, my step granddaughter, calls me Mom-Mom. One day I took Marlee and Andrew to see Santa Claus. Santa Claus said to both of them, 'I bet you love your grandma.' Andrew got very angry and said, 'That's my Grandmom, and it's her Mom-Mom.' That speaks to the special relationships I have with both Marlee and Andrew.

When Andrew's parents were getting divorced, Mindy and I were very close and Ron is like a son to me. You have to be a grown-up and not get caught up in the kids' stuff. There should be one place where life converges for the kids. Now Mindy has two daughters with her second husband, but I'm just Andrew's Grandmom. The relationship defines everything when they are not yours by birth. Because you are the grandmother, doesn't a grandmother make and visa versa. It is not about writing checks or buying presents, it's about time—time—time and the quality of what you put into that time."

For the last twenty years, I have been a Chosen Granny-Nanny. After my divorce from my first husband, I dated a man for ten years whose son and daughter-in-law gave birth to two sons. From the beginning, Peter and Patti (the parents) considered me Nicholas and Bennett's grandmother. Both Peter and Patti's mothers had died before the birth of their sons. Both Bennett and Nicholas call me "Grandma Lo-Lo," and it is more than just a name. From the day they were each born, my house was the first place they had a sleepover without their parents. I was always the primary baby-sitter. Even after Peter and Patti had moved to California, and Peter's father and I stopped dating, they called me to come stay with the boys while they went on a second honeymoon. I, of course, went willingly, and had a marvelous week of bonding and taking care of Nicholas and Bennett. Even today, both boys are grown, and I have three biological grandsons of my own and one step-grand-daughter—but I am still their "Grandma Lo-Lo." Once a year they come to my house for several days, and I look forward to these annual visits. What started as a request that I be the chosen Granny-Nanny has turned into a lasting bond and much joy!

Actually, I learned how to be a Granny-Nanny because of Nicholas and Bennett. The love I feel for them is strong and powerful. I joke about being destined to have mostly grandsons now that my two sons each have three sons between them. I have a total of five grandsons, plus my step-grand-daughter, Rachael. I don't think of myself as having three grandsons, but five! The bond that was created with Nicholas and Bennett, which began as a choice, hasn't weakened because of the addition of my own biological grandsons and a step-granddaughter. The geographic distance between Nicholas, Bennett and me is the factor that is the most difficult barrier to overcome.

A true Chosen Granny-Nanny takes her role seriously. If your intention is just to be a nominal chosen grandmother, then you don't qualify for the title of Chosen Granny-Nanny.

When I am out with Nicholas and Bennett they refer to me as their grandmother. I refer to them as my grandsons, both publicly and in my heart. If you can't fulfill the role, don't take on the relationship. Just because you may be flattered by a request to fill in as a chosen grandmother doesn't mean you should accept the role unless you mean to live up to the title!

17

"My Son Is My Granddaughter's Uncle"

Or

Unusual Situations

The most unusual case I came across was the relationship between Sybil T, who lives in Israel, and her 38 year-old daughter. Sybil has 6 children ranging from age 15 to 38. When Sybil was pregnant with her last child, a son, her daughter was pregnant with her first child, a daughter. The two babies were born very close together. Both mothers were breast-feeding. Sybil taught at a university where her daughter was a student. When her daughter was attending classes and unable to breast-feed, Sybil breast-fed her granddaughter. Likewise, when Sybil was unable to breastfeed and had to teach, her daughter breast-fed Sybil's son (her daughter's brother). Strange? True. When the two children were ready for nursery school they decided to send them to the same school. The first day Sybil's granddaughter said to the teacher, "I want to sit next to my uncle!" The teacher corrected her and said, "You mean your cousin, honey." "No," said Sybil's granddaughter. "He's my uncle."

When I asked Sybil T. how many grandchildren she had she replied, "I have adopted my late mother-in-law's response that I don't count grandchildren, but the distribution is as follows: My oldest daughter is married for a second time. She has two daughters, 15 and 12, from her first marriage; a son, 2 ½ and a newborn daughter from her second marriage, and two daughters 13 and 11, (who spend several months a year with them) from her second husband's first marriage. They are all my grandchildren. My younger daughter has a daughter, almost 11 months old, and my son has a daughter almost 7 months old. My daughters live around 15 minutes away by car. My married son lives about an hour and a half away. And of course, my one daughter and I each had a baby around the same time—and that is another story."

Not every grandmother/daughter duo has such an unusual story, but I did encounter other cases such as that of Betty B., who said, "I feel very fortunate having had only one child and now I have three grandchildren. My daughter had her first child at the same age that I had her—at twenty-four years of age. I would like to have my grandchildren more but my daughter is very possessive and restrictive. I think in some way that she is getting back at me because she thinks I was not always there for her. I was a single mom and it was just the two of us. It is hard now for her to let them go. Her immediate reaction is no. I am always trying to get things to lure my grandchildren to my house. I feel there's great competition between us. My daughter feels like I am competing with her for her children. I am trying to be a better grandmother than she is a mother. I care about the kids so much and I want to introduce them to things they don't get from their parents."

Clearly, Betty and her daughter have some unfinished issues that influence how much Betty is allowed to be with her grandchildren. Betty feels that her daughter is punishing her by not letting the grandchildren spend more time with her.

The mother/daughter relationship continues even after the grandchildren are born. Even though most grandmothers felt that the maternal grandmothers had an edge over the paternal grandmothers, a lot depends on the mother/daughter relationship.

Of course, the same can be said about the mother/son relationship and how it affects the grandmother's relationship with her grandchildren. Helene S., a 64-year-old mother of 3 daughters and one son is the paternal grandmother of 4-year-old Samantha. Because of a family rift and a legal matter, which has torn the family apart, Helene almost never sees her granddaughter. Before that she saw her by going to New Jersey every week or every other week. But now Helene's son (and her daughters) won't speak with her, and she is banned from seeing her granddaughter. Helene said, "I miss seeing my granddaughter because it's natural and I'm very family and relationship conscious. I don't see her because I can't, and I talk myself into saying it's okay. The last time I saw Samantha was a year ago, and now we don't even talk. I feel that once in a while my daughter-in-law could call and update me, but she's a mouse and afraid to alienate my son (her husband). It's either part of my life or it isn't. When I talk about it (which is seldom) it seems like I'm talking about somebody else. I hope it gets better. They are welcome in my life regardless. The truth is I avoid confrontation, and since this terrible family disagreement there is no contact. It all depends on my son and my relationship with him. My hope lies in the fact that I see this getting better. I don't even talk to any of my daughters, and I know girls need their mother, but there's nothing I can do. As a divorced grandmother I was fine if my ex was there when I did see Samantha but he wasn't fine around me. I used to send things to Samantha when I couldn't see her but then they started sending the gifts back unopened. But I have moved on in my life. I have to."

Helene's situation is very complex and involves some legal complications after the death of her own mother. Helene has learned to live with the pain of not being involved in her granddaughter's life (or the lives of any of her three daughters and son). She believes she has to move on with her own life since there is nothing she can do at this point to make it different with her children.

Clearly, a mother's relationship with her own children strongly influences the role she can or cannot play in her grandchildren's lives. Even though most grandmothers felt that the maternal grandmothers had an edge over the paternal grandmothers, a lot depends on the mother/child relationship. Mothers and daughters who are alienated or mothers and sons who are alienated both have a major impact on the family for many generations, and immediately impact on the relationship between the grandmother and her grandchildren (the children of her child).

18

Live-In Granny-Nanny

There are two types of live-in Granny-Nannies: one category is where the Granny-Nanny's home houses her grandchildren and perhaps her children too, and the other is where the Granny-Nanny lives in her children's home with the grandchildren (3 generation household).

In both cases one of the best things about grandmothering is not possible, that is, being able to send the grandkids home once the fun's over. So how do those Granny-Nannies fare who are raising their grandchildren full-time as surrogate parents? Interesting question since there are about 4 million grandchildren living under their grandmother's roof. A recent study by Maximiliane E. Szinovacz, Stanley DeViney and Maxine P. Atkinson sheds some light on what life is like in those households. The study, reported in the Journal of Gerontology: Social Sciences, looked at the Granny-Nannies who were raising their grandchildren in their homes.

One finding was that these grandmothers take the main burden of childcare, and this burden apparently leads to stress symptoms. Long-term stays of grandchildren seem to be particularly difficult when the grandchild's mother is also in the household. In many cases the grandmother is left scrambling for extra cash to cover additional food, clothing, medical and legal expenses. But these Granny-Nannies wouldn't have it any other way. Even when tired, depressed, and confused, she smiles and deals with it day by day.

She's often doing it because of the pride in taking care of your own. Although grandmothers raising grandchildren isn't a recent phenomena, an Administration for Aging fact sheet states that instances of children growing up in homes maintained by their grandparents have grown steadily—up 76 percent from 2.2 million in 1970 to 3.9 million in 1997. Reasons for grandparents raising grandchildren range from death of parents, incarceration, unemployment, substance abuse, teen pregnancy, family violence, to HIV/AIDS. Usually not a single problem puts grandchildren in the care of their grandparents, but rather a combination.

It may be different for the Granny-Nannies who move in with their children and grandchildren. Reasons for this vary from recent widowhood, the inability to afford housing of her own, health reasons (where a grandmother needs her own children to care for her) and needing Grandma around when both parents work or when one grandchild has special needs and Granny-Nanny's extra help is needed.

Penelope N, a 74 year-old who is Granny-Nanny to her daughter's 3 children and her son's two children, has recently been living in her daughter's household. Two of her daughter's children live on their own since graduating from college, and a teen-age girl in high school is still living at home. Penelope has been living with her daughter, son-in-law, and granddaughter for the past 3 months after she was diagnosed with a recurrence of breast cancer. Initially she had come up for a long visit, during which she went for a physical examination and learned of the recurrence. Since then she has been receiving treatments while living with her daughter. Penelope has a home in Florida, and during the past several years, all of her family has spent a month visiting her in the summer and during the winter holiday season. This year, however, her summer plans have changed and she is living in Philadelphia with her daughter's family.

Penelope N. said, "When I was a long-distance Grandmother I was more involved with my daughter Judy's children, and they were younger. As they get older you have to keep your distance. My granddaughter Ariel is much more grown-up, and I don't see her day after day even though I'm now living in their house. She'll be back, though. I remember when her older sister Jessica was a teenager and after college when she left home, and I said that she'd be back. Jessica and I don't talk very often but there's a very special feeling between us. At that time Judy was in the middle of separating from her first husband, and Jessica was with me. But when Jessica was a teenager she separated herself for a while. But they all come back if you have a good relationship with them.

"Now that I am living in my daughter's home I see my granddaughter Ariel, who is the only one still living at home. I see her too much, I guess. Judy and I are very close. I have always felt love from her kids. Sometimes I forget that Judy is grown-up. Now that I'm at their house I sometimes have to be careful. I sometimes intervene with Ariel and if she gets angry she'll get over it. But now I'm living here and it's hard for me because my mother lived with us and it was difficult, and I always said I didn't want to do that to my kids. I don't want my kids to be responsible for me. It's hard now—I've never done this before. It's very hard on me because I don't want to be in the way. My daughter says it's easier for her this way because if I had gone back to Florida she'd just worry about me. I guess her attitude filtered down to her kids. I never had any grandparents so I didn't know what was required, but I love my children and my grandchildren, and I'm especially close to my daughter's children."

Penelope obviously goes out of her way not to be intrusive while she's living in her daughter's household. Her wonderful, close relationship with her daughter makes it easier. Penelope admits that it's easier when they are at her home in Florida, then she doesn't feel like she's intrusive or in the way.

Gertrude G, a Granny-Nanny in her 80's, had her daughter, son-in-law and grandchildren living in her house for seven years. Gertrude said, "My daughter Andrea was in her ninth month of pregnancy. They had a house, and her husband John tore it apart and until it was fixed they couldn't live in it. So in Andrea's 9th month she moved in with us and lived with me when her first son was born. She was still at my house two and a half years later when she was pregnant with her second son. Both Andrea and John worked full-time, and I was the caretaker since I was home. I have had a big hand in raising my grandsons, and we're very close and loving since I was with them for the first seven years. Andrea would get sitters to help me when they weren't home. I was always very much a part of their life. When Doug was 7 years old they all moved back into their house. But still I picked up the boys after school every day and fed them dinner. You do have to live close enough to them to interact like that. When I was a kid, daughters who married might live next store to their mothers so the grandkids had 2 houses next store to each other.

"I am very close to my daughter. Since they lived in my house I baby-proofed my house—put things away, put locks on cabinets, blocked the electrical sockets. Having my children and raising them was always a joy for me. Family is an important part of my life. That doesn't mean that when they were living in my house that there weren't some times that I thought—'I did this already!' when I was annoyed, but it all melted away in a little while. Usually I was just tired at the time. But the years they lived in my house built a bond, a strong bond for me with my two grandsons.

"My son has children, and they live in New Jersey. He married a woman with a daughter. Then my son and his wife Angela had a baby, my granddaughter Dory. Now that Dory is 9 years old I email her. I started sending her emails when she was 7. It's a great way to connect. I try to go every other Sunday and take them all out for brunch. Angela is a loving daughter-in-law, and she loves to entertain. She enjoys it when we come to their house. Without a doubt, however, because of the 7 years that my daughter's family lived in my house, I have a super strong bond with those two boys."

Florence W., a 73 year old Granny-Nanny from Lansdale, Pennsylvania, is the mother of three daughters and the grandmother of three granddaughters ages 20, 18 and 15, and a grandson Dylan who is almost two years old. Florence's daughter Jill and Jill's daughter Rachael lived in Florence's house from the time Rachael was three until she was eleven years old (a total of eight years). Jill had left her husband, and, said Florence; "We wouldn't have wanted it any other way. We'd seen other women trying to get along alone with a child, and we felt they were safe with us and would be well fed. Because of living with us, Jill was able to go to school because we could stay with Rachael. Jill was also able to work on weekends and go to college during the week. She was able to do it because we were here to baby-sit. She got her degree—and all of that was a credit to her—she was determined, hard working and safe in our house. If she hadn't been with us she might not have been able to do all that. Of course, Jill and I get along well together so there was never anything unpleasant between us.

"Rachael and I have bonded to this day, even though she's eighteen now. Just the other day Rachael sat beside me on the couch and snuggled up with her head on my shoulder and fell asleep. Teenagers can be awful, but they are really not awful. Even our oldest granddaughter (now 20) still stops in to see us—even if it's only for 5 minutes. I'm very lucky because all of my grandchildren live near me. And Dylan is the first boy in my family in 44 years.

"I don't speak to Jill everyday. I think that's over doing it. I think that if they want to talk to me they will call me. She knows, as all my family knows, I am behind my daughter through everything and my grandchildren too. Those special years when Jill and Rachael lived with us forged a bond that will always be there. I would do it all again. I wouldn't want it any other way!"

Elmira H., a working class Granny-Nanny in her early seventies, has 8 children, 6 grandchildren and many great-grandchildren. Her daughter and her grandchildren grew up in her house where today her 22-year-old granddaughter and 34-year-old grandson still live. Elmira herself was an only child. She is without a mother or father and said, "There's only me. I was an only child. I like it now. It's nice. I enjoy them and love them. It's me and my kids and my grandchildren. We are all we have, I tell them. And we're a loving family." Her own sons are out of the house on their own. My grandkids from my daughter grew up in my house, and the 22 and 34 year old are still here. To me they are my kids, like the sisters and brothers I never had. Economically it's easier for my kids and grandchildren to live with me. When they were small I did all the cooking. When my older daughter was a mother we both cooked. Though I always did most of the cooking. They all love my cooking. My one granddaughter Tiffany is now on her own and got herself a house. She called and wants me to do all the cooking for her house warming. When I hesitated she said, 'Please, Grandma, I love your cooking.' So I agreed to do it. If you have a family try to be close to them. Now-a-days kids aren't close to their mothers. I teach them that we're one happy family, and that I'm here for them. Their father is gone, but I will always be here for them. It's wonderful for me."

Then there are four-generation households. Vera D., a 71-year-old Granny-Nanny living in Merion, Pennsylvania, has four generations living in her home. Vera's mother is 92 with Alzheimers and lives in Vera and her husband's home, as do her daughter and her granddaughter Michelle. Michelle has been living in Vera's house for two years. Prior to that her other granddaughter, now in college, lived there on and off. Both granddaughters are the children of Vera's daughter, an only child.

Vera D. said, "My daughter was working in Maryland when her daughter Michelle came to live with me. My daughter found it difficult to work with a 7-year-old to care for, so Michelle came to live with me. My daughter and I love each other dearly, but she's a free spirit and we used to butt heads. Then 2 months ago, my daughter lost her job in Maryland and came to live with us too. I guess we've both mellowed. I gave my daughter two or three things to do to make my life better, and we try to work things out and let each other know if something bothers either of us. My daughter has turned out to be a big help with my mother, who cannot feed or dress herself. My daughter has been a big help, especially with the heavy physical labor of lifting and moving my mother. And my granddaughters are very caring and loving with my mother. When they come in they hug and kiss her. Things are working very well for us now, better than I ever expected. There are a lot of us here but everybody is trying in a relaxed way to make life a little easier. We all understand that our life is now crowded but better. I have a big house so we each can find space to go off to be by ourselves. My daughter has turned out to be a blessing. I'm getting older and my daughter does a lot of the heavy physical things for my mother. She is very helpful. We work together—different generations working together. I think my granddaughter Michelle sees her mother in a different light—as more sharing and giving. I have a strong bond with my granddaughter. We had a July family reunion—a 5-day cruise to Nova Scotia. My daughter said she'd stay home and take care of my mother. My husband didn't want to go, and my older granddaughter couldn't go. So Michelle said she'd go and the two of us had a wonderful time.

"Of course, sometimes they mess up my kitchen after I've cleaned it. We started out that I'd do the breakfast and lunch dishes and they would do the dinner dishes. Then sometimes I'd get busy with something and it would get backed up. What we do then is we all pitch in and help. They're learning to do things the way I like it. If they try it's acceptable to me. We're trying to mesh. Some nights, however, I'm tired and then next time my daughter's tired—so we cooperate. My granddaughter Michelle had my rules when she lived with us without her mother. Now with her mother here too rules change. But at last we're banding together so Michelle doesn't play one of us against the other to bend the rules. Of course, I would like my daughter to have a stable home of her own and independence. But now I realize that I manage better with her help so it's better than I expected. When my daughter does go her own way, I'll have to adjust so I keep it in the back of my mind so I don't get totally dependent on her. Before I retired I thought I'd go to this place or classes, but life turned out differently. It's like trying to accept Altzheimers. You stop the struggle and accommodate and work around it. Actually, this is what I want to do. I'm 71, and I want to get as much pleasure out of life as possible. If I focus on the negatives I won't. I can figure out the way around difficulties, and not focus on the negatives. I try to get joy and pleasure out of life. Having 4 generations living together has turned out to be a joy and a big help for all of us—for my daughter and my granddaughter, and for me as I care for my 91 year old mother."

The Granny-Nannies whose grandchildren lived in their home seemed to feel happier about the arrangement, while the Granny-Nannies who lived with their grandchildren in the homes of their children were more worried about being in the way, or a burden, or a nuisance.

All the live-in Granny-Nannies with whom I spoke felt a special bond with those grandchildren. The day-to-day contact, the interpersonal interaction, all helped to build a very close bond between these grandmothers and grandchildren.

19

Conclusions

Granny-Nanny, take your role seriously because you have a lot to give. Be a consistent presence in your grandchildren's lives. Baby-sit regularly or when needed. Lavish special attention on your grandchildren. Not only will it help your grandchildren grow, but at the same time you'll win the eternal gratitude of your children who need some downtime.

In between visits, fill in the gaps with weekly telephone calls to each child. Encourage each grandchild to share a "news" item with you. Use videotapes to keep in touch. Exchange letters, packages, drawings. Your positive feedback will help build their self-esteem.

Look forward to holidays to create memories that make your family close. Encourage everyone to celebrate them at your house.

The constant contact with your grandchildren teaches you how to really listen to them, to understand what they mean to say, not just the words they use. When you take your grandchildren's words seriously and respect their opinions, they will let you know what is going on in their lives. It will strengthen the growing bonds between you and your grandchild. Christina Ianzito in the July/August 2002 issue of AARP in her article "Embracing the Future" writes about the new "AARP Grandparent Study." One-third of the grandparents surveyed said they enjoy spoiling their grandkids, but the majority (about 83 percent) think their real responsibility to the kids involves instilling strong values.

"Grandparents aren't in this just for the fun of it," says Amy Goyer, coordinator of AARP's Grandparent Information Center. "They take their grandparenting duties very seriously."

The GIC-sponsored study also found that for those surveyed being a grandparent means:

Opening Your Wallet The average grandparent spends about $500 a year on the grandkids. About half say they help pay for their grandchildren's education, and 45 percent say they assist with living expenses. In addition, about 15 percent of the grandparents surveyed provide some level of daycare for their grandchildren—up from 8 percent in 1998.

Giving Your Time The most common activity grandparents say they've shared with their grandkids in the past six months is a dinner together. Other popular pastimes: watching TV, reading aloud, and shopping.

Staying In Touch Almost 70 percent of grandparents manage to see their grandchildren at least once every week or two, and one-quarter spend time with them at least once every few months. The task is harder for some grandparents because they live far away or their grandkids have busy schedules. When a face-to-face visit isn't possible, they're far more likely to use the telephone than the mouse: 65 percent of grandparents say they never send e-mail to their grandchildren.

Luckiest are grandparents in their 60s: 62 percent of them report seeing their grandchildren at least once a week. Only 55 percent of grandparents in their 50s and 70s can make the same claim.

Of course, people can't call themselves "grand" until they've been plain old parents first. And it is in that role that they lay the foundation for a fulfilling grandparenthood. The study found that," grandparents who have a good relationship with their own children are more likely to feel good about being grandparents," says GIC manager Jane King.

As a result of the interviews conducted for this book, some unexpected findings emerged:

1. Most of the grandmothers interviewed felt that the maternal grandmothers had a distinct advantage over the paternal grandmothers based on the very fact that the mothers, by and large, relied on their own mothers, the maternal granny-nannies, before they turned to their mothers-in-law, the paternal granny-nannies.

2. Proximity to a granny-nanny's grandchildren also impacts the closeness between a granny-nanny and her grandchildren. Granny-nannies who live near their grandchildren have the time and frequency and more chances to bond and to be together spontaneously as opposed to long-distance grandmothering which is less frequent and requires travel time and usually advance planning.

3. The question of self-esteem only came up for families of minority groups such as Jewish families or African-American families. These

granny-nannies saw their roles as including helping their grandchildren develop self-esteem—something that did not come up in the interviews with white Christian granny-nannies.

4. Consistency and rituals help the bonding process. Granny-Nannies who were a consistent presence in their grandchildren's lives and who shared rituals such as holidays and birthdays together were more bonded than granny-nannies who were a more haphazard presence in their grandchildren's lives.

5. The relationship between a granny-nanny and the parents of the grandchildren influenced the closeness between a granny-nanny and her grandchildren. Tension among the older set of parent and child usually greatly erodes the relationship between the granny-nanny and her grandchildren. In other words, a granny-nanny's relationship with her own children strongly influences the role she can play in her grandchildren's lives.

6. A baby friendly granny-nanny's house is far more welcoming than a pristine, "don't touch" house, and a grandchild will think of Grandma's house as his or her second home if it is child friendly.

7. Parents trust granny-nannies who follow their rules and don't do things their own way, even when it conflicts with the parent's way. Such a Granny-Nanny will develop a closer relationship with her grandchildren and her own child's family. The parents of the grandchildren are in charge, even when the granny-nanny is babysitting.

8. Overall, grandmothers I interviewed agreed that the most valuable time they spend with a grandchild is one-on-one time. Often that means taking each grandchild alone for a special day.

9. Both divorce and parent/child relationships have a stronger impact on the granny-nanny's relationship with her grandchildren than geographic proximity.

So, Granny-Nannies, you're on your way to being a superb grandmother. Start with making sure your relationship with your child/the parent is sound and any unfinished business is taken care of so that you can move on to the Granny-Nanny role.

You have been given a unique opportunity to enrich your life and the lives of your children and grandchildren and their entire extended families. Don't blow it! Make some conscious decisions, make some focused time, and give unselfishly of your love.

Lois Young-Tulin
5 Curtis Park Drive
Wyncote, PA 19095

(215) 884-7324

E-mail: youngtulin@aol.com

978-0-595-35188-6
0-595-35188-3

Printed in the United States
95911LV00005BA/328/A

9 780595 351886